International Relations in a Flash

The Absolute Essentials & Principles of Understanding
Global Power Dynamics, Diplomacy, and World Affairs

Joseph Goldstein

This book is designed to provide general information regarding the topics discussed. It is offered with the understanding that neither the author nor the publisher is engaged in rendering financial, legal, or other professional advice. While efforts have been made to ensure the accuracy and reliability of the information contained in this publication, the author and publisher do not guarantee its accuracy or completeness and shall not be responsible for any errors, omissions, or for the results obtained from the use of such information. The material in this book is provided "as is," without any express or implied warranties.

Readers are encouraged to consult a qualified professional for advice tailored to their personal or professional situation. The strategies and information discussed may not be appropriate for every situation and are not promised or guaranteed to produce specific outcomes. Neither the author nor the publisher will be liable for any loss, damage, or other consequences that may arise from the use of or reliance on the information provided.

No representation is made about the quality of information provided exceeding that obtainable through professional advice. In no event will the author or publisher be responsible for any direct, indirect, incidental, consequential, or other damages resulting from the use of the information in this book.

PREFACE

Welcome to "International Relations in a Flash – The Absolute Essentials & Principles of Understanding Global Power Dynamics, Diplomacy, and World Affairs"! If you've ever felt overwhelmed by the complexity of global politics or struggled to make sense of the daily news about international events, you're not alone. The world of international relations can seem like a tangled web of treaties, conflicts, and power struggles. This book is here to help you unravel that web and gain a clear understanding of how our world works on the global stage.

We've distilled years of academic research, diplomatic history, and current events into a concise, easy-to-digest format. Our goal is to give you the essential knowledge you need to understand global affairs, without drowning you in jargon or overwhelming detail.

Why is this book important? In our increasingly interconnected world, understanding international relations isn't just for diplomats and politicians anymore. Whether you're a student, a business professional, or simply a curious citizen, having a grasp on global dynamics can help you make sense of the world around you. It can inform your decisions, from how you vote to where you invest your money. Plus, it's just plain fascinating!

Here's what you can expect from this book:

1. **Clear, concise explanations**: We've broken down complex theories and historical events into bite-sized pieces that are easy to understand and remember. Each chapter and section of the book is designed to stand on its own for those who prefer to pick and choose what they'd prefer to read.
2. **Real-world relevance**: Throughout the book, we'll show you how abstract concepts play out in current events and everyday life.
3. **A balanced perspective**: International relations is full of competing theories and viewpoints. We'll present multiple sides of key debates, encouraging you to think critically and form your own opinions.
4. **A thorough overview**: From traditional topics like diplomacy and war to emerging issues like cybersecurity and global health, we cover the full spectrum of international relations.
5. **Future-focused thinking**: We'll not only explain how we got to where we are today, but also explore where we might be heading in the future of global politics.

As you go through this book, remember that international relations isn't just about faraway capitals and high-level negotiations. It's about people – billions of them – and how their lives are shaped by decisions made on the global stage. It's about the food you eat, the clothes you wear, the technology you use, and the air you breathe. It's about our shared challenges and our collective hopes for the future.

We've designed this book to be accessible whether you're completely new to the subject or looking to refresh your knowledge. Feel free to dive in from the beginning or jump to specific chapters that interest you most. Each chapter builds on the others, but can also stand alone as a quick reference guide.

By the time you finish this book, you'll have a solid foundation in international relations. You'll be able to analyze news events with a more informed perspective, engage in meaningful discussions about global issues, and perhaps even see your own role in the world a bit differently.

TOPICAL OUTLINE

Chapter 1: Introduction to International Relations

- Definition and Scope of International Relations
- Key Actors in Global Politics
- The Role of Sovereignty and Statehood
- Anarchy and the International System
- Power and Influence in Global Affairs
- The Balance of Power Theory
- Realism vs. Idealism in IR
- The Impact of Globalization on IR
- Non-State Actors: NGOs, IGOs, and Multinational Corporations
- The Evolution of International Relations as a Discipline

Chapter 2: Theories of International Relations

- Realism and Neorealism
- Liberalism and Neoliberalism
- Constructivism in International Relations
- Marxism and Critical Theories
- Feminist Theories in International Relations

Chapter 3: Global Governance and Institutions

- The United Nations and its Role
- International Law and Treaties
- Global Economic Institutions (IMF, World Bank, WTO)
- Regional Organizations (EU, ASEAN, African Union)

Chapter 4: Diplomacy and Negotiation

- History and Evolution of Diplomacy
- Types of Diplomacy (Bilateral, Multilateral, Track II)
- The Art of Negotiation in IR
- The Role of Diplomats and Embassies

Chapter 5: Security Studies in International Relations

- Traditional vs. Non-Traditional Security
- The Concept of National Security
- Global Terrorism and Counterterrorism Strategies
- Nuclear Proliferation and Arms Control
- Cybersecurity as a New Dimension of Security

Chapter 6: Conflict and Cooperation in International Relations

- Causes of International Conflicts
- War and Peace Theories
- Conflict Resolution and Peacebuilding
- Alliances and Collective Security

Chapter 7: The Global Economy and International Trade

- Theories of International Trade
- Globalization and its Economic Impact
- Trade Agreements and Economic Integration
- The Role of Multinational Corporations

Chapter 8: International Political Economy

- Economic Theories in IR (Mercantilism, Liberalism, Marxism)
- Globalization and Inequality
- The Role of International Financial Markets
- Development and Poverty Alleviation
- Economic Sanctions and Their Political Impacts

Chapter 9: Human Rights and Humanitarian Issues

- The Evolution of Human Rights in IR
- Human Rights Violations and Global Responses
- The Role of International Humanitarian Organizations
- Humanitarian Intervention and the Responsibility to Protect (R2P)

Chapter 10: Environmental Issues in International Relations

- Climate Change and Global Environmental Policies
- International Environmental Agreements
- Sustainable Development in IR
- The Politics of Natural Resources
- Transboundary Environmental Issues (e.g., Water Sharing, Air Pollution)

Chapter 11: Regional Conflicts and Global Impacts

- The Middle East and International Politics
- Asian Geopolitics and Power Struggles
- Africa's Role in Global Affairs
- Latin American Politics and International Relations

Chapter 12: The Role of Technology in International Relations

- Cybersecurity and Global Politics
- The Impact of Social Media on Diplomacy
- Technological Warfare and Defense Systems
- Global Communication Networks and Diplomacy
- Space Exploration and International Cooperation

Chapter 13: International Relations in the Post-Cold War Era

- The End of the Cold War and its Global Impact
- Unipolarity vs. Multipolarity
- The Rise of China and Emerging Powers
- The Role of the United States in the New World Order

Chapter 14: Global Health and International Relations

- The Impact of Global Pandemics
- International Health Organizations (WHO, CDC)
- Health Diplomacy and Global Cooperation
- Access to Medicines and Global Health Inequities

Chapter 15: Ethics and Morality in International Relations

- Moral Dilemmas in Global Politics
- Ethical Theories in IR
- The Ethics of War and Peace
- Humanitarian Ethics and Global Intervention

Chapter 16: Future Trends in International Relations

- The Impact of AI and Automation on Global Politics
- The Future of Global Governance
- Challenges to International Order
- Prospects for Global Peace and Security

Appendix

- Terms and Definitions

Afterword

TABLE OF CONTENTS

Chapter 1: Introduction to International Relations ... 1

Chapter 2: Theories of International Relations ... 20

Chapter 3: Global Governance and Institutions ... 29

Chapter 4: Diplomacy and Negotiation ... 39

Chapter 5: Security Studies in International Relations ... 47

Chapter 6: Conflict and Cooperation in International Relations ... 56

Chapter 7: The Global Economy and International Trade ... 63

Chapter 8: International Political Economy ... 70

Chapter 9: Human Rights and Humanitarian Issues ... 79

Chapter 10: Environmental Issues in International Relations ... 86

Chapter 11: Regional Conflicts and Global Impacts ... 95

Chapter 12: The Role of Technology in International Relations ... 103

Chapter 13: International Relations in the Post-Cold War Era ... 111

Chapter 14: Global Health and International Relations ... 118

Chapter 15: Ethics and Morality in International Relations ... 123

Chapter 16: Future Trends in International Relations ... 129

Appendix ... 135

Afterword ... 138

CHAPTER 1: INTRODUCTION TO INTERNATIONAL RELATIONS

Definition and Scope of International Relations

International Relations (IR) examines the interactions between nations, focusing on how they cooperate, compete, and conflict. It's about understanding the behavior of states and other actors on the global stage. When we talk about IR, we're delving into a wide range of activities and issues that transcend national borders. This field explores how countries establish relationships through diplomacy, trade, and treaties, and how they deal with challenges like war, peace, and economic inequality.

At its core, IR studies the conduct of states. States, or countries, are the primary actors, but they're not the only ones. Other entities, like international organizations (e.g., the United Nations), non-governmental organizations (NGOs), multinational corporations, and even influential individuals, play significant roles. The relationships between these actors form a complex web that IR seeks to understand.

One key aspect of IR is the concept of **sovereignty**. Sovereignty refers to the authority of a state to govern itself without external interference. This principle is central to how countries interact, as it shapes the boundaries of influence and control. However, sovereignty can also lead to conflicts, especially when one state's actions impact another's autonomy.

Diplomacy is another fundamental element of IR. It's the practice of negotiation between states, aiming to resolve disputes without resorting to conflict. Diplomats work to represent their countries' interests, engage in discussions, and forge agreements that can maintain or restore peace. **Diplomacy is often seen as the art of compromise**, where the goal is to find a solution that satisfies all parties involved.

Trade and economics also fall within the scope of IR. Countries trade goods, services, and capital across borders, which influences their relationships. Economic policies, tariffs, sanctions, and aid are tools used by states to achieve their foreign policy objectives. For instance, economic sanctions can be used as a non-military means to pressure a state into changing its behavior. The global economy is interlinked, and the actions of one country can have ripple effects across the world. Understanding these economic interactions is crucial for comprehending the broader dynamics of IR.

Security is a major concern in IR, encompassing both military and non-military aspects. National security involves protecting a state's citizens, economy, and institutions from external threats. This can include military defense against invasions or terrorist attacks. However, security isn't just about military power. Environmental issues, pandemics, and cyber threats also pose significant risks. IR examines how states and international organizations address these threats and work together to enhance global security.

IR also covers **conflict and peace**. Wars, both past and present, have shaped the international system. Understanding the causes of conflict, whether they're territorial disputes, ideological clashes, or resource competitions, is vital. IR explores not only why conflicts occur but also how they can be prevented or resolved. Peace studies, a subfield of IR, focuses on the conditions necessary for sustainable peace, such as economic development, human rights, and political stability.

Human rights have become an increasingly important aspect of IR. The international community has developed norms and treaties to protect individuals' rights, regardless of where they live. However, enforcing these rights remains a challenge. IR examines how states and international bodies respond to human rights violations and the tension between state sovereignty and global ethical standards.

Global governance is another critical area within IR. As the world becomes more interconnected, issues like climate change, pandemics, and transnational crime require collective action. No single country can tackle these problems alone. Global governance refers to the institutions, rules, and agreements that guide international cooperation. Organizations like the United Nations, World Trade Organization, and International Monetary Fund are central to this process, helping to coordinate efforts and manage global issues.

Theories in IR provide frameworks for understanding these complex interactions. Realism, liberalism, and constructivism are three dominant theories. Realism focuses on the idea that states are primarily concerned with their own survival and power. Liberalism, on the other hand, emphasizes the role of international institutions and cooperation. Constructivism looks at how ideas, identities, and norms shape international relations. Each theory offers a different perspective on how the world works, and they're often used in combination to explain international events.

IR also considers the role of **non-state actors**, such as terrorist groups, multinational corporations, and NGOs. These actors can influence international policies and outcomes, sometimes even more than states themselves. For example, multinational corporations can affect global trade patterns, and NGOs can shape international norms and human rights agendas.

Finally, IR is not just about what happens between states; it's also about how global issues affect individuals. Globalization has made the world more connected, but it has also brought challenges like inequality and cultural clashes. IR explores how these global trends impact everyday lives, shaping the world in which we all live.

In essence, International Relations is about understanding the complex and ever-changing world of global interactions. It covers a broad spectrum of topics, from diplomacy and trade to security and human rights, offering insights into how the world works and how it might be improved.

Key Actors in Global Politics

Global politics is shaped by a variety of actors, each playing distinct roles on the international stage. These actors include states, international organizations, non-governmental organizations (NGOs), multinational corporations (MNCs), and even influential individuals. Understanding the dynamics between these actors is crucial to comprehending global political interactions.

States are the primary actors in global politics. A state, defined by its sovereignty and government, holds the authority to govern its population and territory. States engage in diplomacy, form alliances, and participate in international organizations to pursue their national interests. The power of a state in global politics is often measured by its economic strength, military capabilities, and political influence. However, not all states hold the same level of power. Superpowers like the United States and China wield significant influence, while smaller states may rely on alliances or international law to protect their interests.

International organizations are another key actor in global politics. These entities, such as the United Nations (UN), World Trade Organization (WTO), and North Atlantic Treaty Organization (NATO), are established by agreements between states. They provide a platform for dialogue, cooperation, and conflict resolution. The UN, for example, plays a vital role in maintaining international peace and security, promoting human rights, and fostering economic development. While international organizations are often seen as neutral actors, their effectiveness depends on the willingness of member states to cooperate and adhere to their rules.

Non-governmental organizations (NGOs) also significantly impact global politics. These organizations operate independently of governments and focus on various issues such as human rights, environmental protection, and humanitarian aid. NGOs like Amnesty International and Greenpeace can influence global politics by raising awareness, shaping public opinion, and pressuring governments to adopt specific policies. They often work closely with international organizations, providing expertise and advocating for policy changes. NGOs' ability to mobilize public support and bring attention to global issues makes them powerful actors, despite lacking formal political power.

Multinational corporations (MNCs) are powerful economic actors in global politics. These companies operate across national borders, influencing global trade, investment, and economic policies. MNCs like Apple, ExxonMobil, and Toyota have revenues that surpass the gross domestic product (GDP) of many states, giving them significant economic leverage. They can shape global politics by lobbying governments, influencing trade agreements, and setting industry standards. However, their pursuit of profit can sometimes lead to conflicts with governments or civil society, especially when their operations impact local communities or the environment.

Influential individuals can also be key actors in global politics. Political leaders like presidents, prime ministers, and monarchs play crucial roles in shaping their countries' foreign policies. Their decisions can have far-reaching consequences for global stability and international relations. For example, the policies of leaders like Vladimir Putin, Xi Jinping, and Joe Biden significantly impact global politics. In addition to political leaders, individuals such as philanthropists, activists, and even celebrities can influence global issues. Figures like Bill Gates, through his foundation, have contributed to global health initiatives, while activists like Malala Yousafzai have raised awareness of education and women's rights globally.

Regional organizations also are important in global politics. These organizations, such as the European Union (EU), African Union (AU), and Association of Southeast Asian Nations (ASEAN), are formed by states within a specific region. They work to promote regional cooperation, economic integration, and political stability. The EU, for example, has created a single market and a common currency (the Euro) and is important in global trade negotiations. Regional organizations can also influence global politics by coordinating collective responses to regional conflicts, economic crises, or environmental challenges.

Non-state actors, such as terrorist groups, armed militias, and transnational criminal organizations, are increasingly influential in global politics. Groups like Al-Qaeda, ISIS, and drug cartels challenge state authority and international security. They operate across borders, using violence and illicit activities to pursue their objectives. While these actors are often viewed as threats, they are an undeniable force in global politics, prompting states and international organizations to develop strategies for countering their influence.

Media and communication networks also play a vital role in global politics. Media organizations, both traditional and digital, shape public perceptions of global events. They influence political agendas by highlighting specific issues, providing platforms for political discourse, and holding governments accountable. Social media has further amplified the role of communication networks, enabling information to spread rapidly and mobilizing public opinion on a global scale. The media can also be used as a tool of propaganda, influencing how states and non-state actors are perceived internationally.

In summary, global politics is not solely the domain of states. A diverse range of actors, including international organizations, NGOs, MNCs, individuals, regional organizations, non-state actors, and media, all contribute to the complex web of interactions that define global politics. Understanding the roles and influence of these actors is essential for anyone seeking to grasp the intricacies of international relations.

The Role of Sovereignty and Statehood

Sovereignty and statehood are foundational concepts in international relations. They define the rights and responsibilities of states and influence how they interact with one another. Sovereignty refers to the authority of a state to govern itself without external interference, while statehood is the status of being recognized as an independent nation-state within the international community.

Sovereignty is the cornerstone of international relations. It grants a state the power to create and enforce laws, control its borders, and conduct foreign policy. This principle is enshrined in the United Nations Charter, which emphasizes the sovereignty of its member states. The idea of sovereignty emerged from the Treaty of Westphalia in 1648, which ended the Thirty Years' War in Europe and established the modern state system. The treaty recognized the authority of states over their territories and marked the beginning of the nation-state as the primary actor in international relations.

Statehood is closely linked to sovereignty. A state must meet specific criteria to be considered sovereign: a defined territory, a permanent population, a functioning government, and the capacity to enter into relations with other states. Recognition by other states is also crucial for statehood. Without recognition, a territory might exist in practice but lack legal standing in the international community. For example, Taiwan operates as an independent state but is not universally recognized due to the One-China policy. As a result, its sovereignty is contested.

The concept of sovereignty is not absolute. **In practice, sovereignty can be challenged or limited.** States may voluntarily cede some aspects of their sovereignty to international organizations or regional bodies. For example, members of the European Union have transferred certain legislative powers to EU institutions to promote integration and cooperation. This pooling of sovereignty allows states to address issues that transcend national borders, such as trade, security, and environmental protection.

Sovereignty can also be challenged by external forces. **Interventions, both military and non-military, are a primary way that state sovereignty is contested.** For instance, humanitarian interventions are sometimes justified on the grounds that a state's actions—or inactions—have led to severe human rights violations. The Responsibility to Protect (R2P) doctrine, endorsed by the UN, argues that the international community has a duty to intervene when a state fails to protect its population from genocide, war crimes, ethnic cleansing, or crimes against humanity. This doctrine creates a tension between respecting state sovereignty and protecting human rights.

Globalization further complicates the concept of sovereignty. **Economic interdependence, technological advancements, and transnational issues** have blurred the lines of sovereignty. States are increasingly affected by decisions made outside their borders, such as international trade agreements, climate change policies, or cybersecurity threats. While states retain their sovereignty, they must navigate a world where their actions are interlinked with those of others. The rise of multinational corporations and global supply chains has also shifted economic power away from states, challenging their control over national economies.

The erosion of sovereignty is also evident in the rise of supranational organizations. These entities, such as the European Union, can make binding decisions on member states, sometimes overriding national laws. Supranationalism represents a significant shift in the traditional understanding of sovereignty, as it involves states voluntarily limiting their sovereignty to achieve common goals. This shift is often controversial, as it raises questions about democratic accountability and the loss of national identity.

Internal challenges to sovereignty are equally significant. **Secessionist movements, civil wars, and internal conflicts** can threaten the sovereignty of a state. When a region within a state seeks independence, it challenges the state's territorial integrity. The cases of Catalonia in Spain and Scotland in the United Kingdom are examples where regional independence movements have sparked debates about the nature of sovereignty and self-determination. Civil wars, such as those in Syria and Yemen, further illustrate how internal conflicts can undermine state sovereignty, leading to state collapse or foreign intervention.

In contrast, sovereignty can also be a tool for states to assert their independence and protect their interests. **National sovereignty is often invoked to resist external pressures or interventions.** States may use the principle of sovereignty to reject international criticism, defend their policies, or maintain control over their natural resources. For example, some countries resist international environmental agreements, arguing that such treaties infringe on their sovereign rights to exploit their resources.

Sovereignty and statehood remain central to international relations. They define the basic framework within which states operate, negotiate, and sometimes conflict.

However, these concepts are constantly evolving, shaped by global changes, internal dynamics, and the ongoing tension between national interests and international cooperation. Understanding the role of sovereignty and statehood is essential for navigating the complexities of global politics.

Anarchy and the International System

Anarchy in the context of international relations doesn't mean chaos or disorder; rather, it refers to the lack of a central authority above states. In the international system, there's no overarching government to enforce rules or resolve conflicts between nations. Each state operates as an independent entity, making decisions based on its own interests, security, and survival. This condition of anarchy is a fundamental characteristic of the international system, shaping the behavior and interactions of states.

In an anarchic international system, **states must rely on themselves for security and survival**. There is no global police force or government to protect states from aggression. As a result, states are concerned with maintaining their sovereignty and territorial integrity. This leads to a focus on military power, alliances, and strategic positioning to deter potential threats. The concept of "self-help" is central in an anarchic system; states must be prepared to defend themselves, as no other actor is guaranteed to come to their aid.

The absence of a central authority also means that **international law and agreements** are not enforced in the same way as laws within a state. While there are international institutions like the United Nations and treaties that set norms and expectations, compliance is largely voluntary. States may choose to follow international rules when it aligns with their interests, but they can also violate these rules if they believe it benefits them. The lack of a higher authority to enforce these rules makes international relations more fluid and unpredictable.

Realist theories of international relations emphasize the role of anarchy in shaping state behavior. According to realism, the anarchic nature of the international system leads states to prioritize power and security above all else. Realists argue that states operate in a perpetual state of competition, where alliances are temporary and the balance of power is crucial for maintaining stability. This perspective views the international system as inherently conflict-prone, with war and competition being natural outcomes of anarchy.

However, anarchy doesn't mean that cooperation is impossible. **Liberal theories** of international relations suggest that despite anarchy, states can work together to achieve common goals. International institutions, trade, and diplomacy are tools that can mitigate the effects of anarchy, leading to more peaceful and cooperative interactions. For instance, the European Union represents a significant example of how states can integrate and cooperate within an anarchic system, reducing the likelihood of conflict.

Constructivist theories offer another perspective, arguing that the meaning of anarchy is shaped by the identities, beliefs, and interactions of states. According to constructivists, anarchy is what states make of it. If states perceive each other as rivals, anarchy will lead to competition and conflict. However, if they view each other as partners, anarchy can foster cooperation and peaceful coexistence. This view highlights the role of social factors in shaping the anarchic system.

Anarchy in the international system creates a complex environment where states must navigate their interests, security, and relationships without a central authority to guide or control them. This condition influences everything from diplomacy and alliances to conflicts and power dynamics, making an understanding of anarchy essential for comprehending global politics.

Power and Influence in Global Affairs

Power and influence are the currencies of global affairs. They determine how states and other actors interact, shape the international system, and achieve their goals. Power in international relations can be understood in multiple ways: as military might, economic strength, political influence, or even soft power like cultural appeal. Understanding how power is acquired, used, and maintained is key to understanding global dynamics.

Military power is one of the most visible and traditional forms of power in global affairs. It involves the ability of a state to defend itself and project force beyond its borders. Countries like the United States, Russia, and China invest heavily in their military capabilities, enabling them to influence global politics through deterrence, alliances, and direct intervention. Military power is not just about having a large army; it includes advanced technology, intelligence, and strategic positioning. For example, the presence of U.S. military bases around the world allows the United States to respond quickly to international crises, influencing events far from its own territory.

However, **economic power** has become increasingly important in global affairs. Economic strength allows states to influence others through trade, investment, and financial aid. Countries with strong economies, such as the United States, China, and Germany, can shape global markets, set trade standards, and offer or withhold economic assistance to influence the behavior of other states. Economic power can be used to impose sanctions, provide development aid, or control critical resources, making it a versatile tool in international relations. For instance, China's Belt and Road Initiative uses economic investments to expand its influence across Asia, Africa, and Europe.

Political influence is another critical aspect of power in global affairs. This involves the ability to shape international norms, institutions, and alliances. States with significant political influence can lead coalitions, set agendas in international organizations, and shape global governance. The United Nations Security Council, where permanent members like the United States, Russia, China, the United Kingdom, and France hold significant sway, is an example of political influence at work. These states can use their positions to shape international law, peacekeeping missions, and responses to global crises.

Beyond military, economic, and political power, **soft power** is important in global affairs. Soft power refers to the ability of a state to influence others through cultural appeal, values, and diplomacy. Countries like the United States have used soft power effectively by promoting democracy, human rights, and cultural products such as movies, music, and technology. Soft power can create goodwill, build alliances, and spread a country's influence without the use of force or coercion. The success of South Korean culture globally, known as the "Korean Wave," is an example of soft power shaping international perceptions and relationships.

Multinational corporations (MNCs) also wield significant power in global affairs. These corporations operate across borders, influencing trade policies, labor standards, and economic development. Companies like Apple, ExxonMobil, and Amazon have revenues larger than the GDPs of many countries, giving them substantial leverage in global markets. MNCs can shape international regulations, lobby governments, and even affect diplomatic relations. Their decisions on where to invest, source materials, or set up operations can have profound impacts on local economies and global supply chains.

International organizations like the United Nations, World Trade Organization, and International Monetary Fund are also key players in global power dynamics. These organizations set rules, resolve disputes, and coordinate global responses to issues like climate change, pandemics, and economic crises. The influence of these organizations depends on the participation and cooperation of member states, but they play a critical role in shaping the international system.

Non-state actors such as NGOs, terrorist groups, and advocacy networks also contribute to power dynamics in global affairs. NGOs can influence international norms and policies through advocacy, research, and public campaigns. For instance, Amnesty International and Human Rights Watch have played crucial roles in highlighting human rights abuses and pressuring governments to change their policies. Terrorist groups like Al-Qaeda and ISIS, though destructive, have also demonstrated how non-state actors can challenge state power and influence global security agendas.

Finally, **alliances and coalitions** are critical mechanisms through which power is exercised in global affairs. States often form alliances to pool their resources, enhance their security, and increase their influence. NATO, for instance, is a military alliance that allows member states to collectively defend against threats, projecting a united front that significantly enhances their combined power. Similarly, economic alliances like the European Union create integrated markets and common policies, amplifying the influence of member states on the global stage.

The Balance of Power Theory

The Balance of Power theory is a cornerstone concept in international relations. It suggests that global stability is maintained when power is distributed among various states in such a way that no single state or coalition can dominate the others. This theory is rooted in the idea that power, particularly military and economic power, needs to be balanced to prevent any one state from becoming too powerful and threatening the security of others.

At the heart of the Balance of Power theory is the belief that states are inherently self-interested. Each state seeks to preserve its sovereignty and security. In an anarchic international system—where there is no overarching authority to enforce rules or protect states—nations must rely on their own capabilities and alliances to ensure their survival. When one state accumulates significant power, it can pose a threat to others, potentially leading to attempts at domination or expansion. To counter this, other states may form alliances or increase their own power to create a balance.

Historically, the Balance of Power theory has been used to explain the behavior of European states, particularly during the 19th century. **The Concert of Europe** is often cited as a classic example of the Balance of Power in action. After the Napoleonic Wars, European powers—such as Britain, France, Austria, Prussia, and Russia—agreed to maintain a balance of power to prevent any one state from becoming too dominant. This system involved shifting alliances and strategic partnerships designed to keep any single power from disrupting the equilibrium. The result was a relatively stable period in Europe, known as the "long peace," which lasted until the outbreak of World War I.

The Balance of Power theory operates on several principles. One key principle is that states will act to prevent any one state from achieving hegemony. If a state becomes too powerful, others will form coalitions to counterbalance it. This often leads to a dynamic and fluid international environment where alliances shift based on changes in power. For example, during the Cold War, the United States and the Soviet Union sought to balance each other's influence globally, leading to a bipolar world where both superpowers tried to prevent the other from gaining too much power.

Another principle is **the concept of deterrence**. States build up their military capabilities to deter others from attacking them. By maintaining a strong defense, a state can discourage aggression, contributing to the overall balance. Deterrence was a crucial component of the Cold War, where the nuclear arms race between the United States and the Soviet Union created a balance of terror. The threat of mutually assured destruction (MAD) kept both superpowers from engaging in direct conflict, thus maintaining a precarious balance.

However, **the Balance of Power theory has its criticisms**. One major criticism is that it can lead to a perpetual state of rivalry and competition, where states are constantly vying for power rather than cooperating. This competition can result in arms races, alliances of convenience, and conflicts of interest that destabilize rather than stabilize the international system. For instance, the alliances formed before World War I, intended to balance power, ultimately contributed to the war's outbreak as states were drawn into the conflict through their obligations to allies.

Another criticism is that the Balance of Power theory may overlook the importance of non-state actors and global institutions. In today's interconnected world, power is not only held by states but also by multinational corporations, international organizations, and other non-state entities. These actors can influence global politics in ways that the traditional Balance of Power theory does not fully account for. Moreover, global challenges such as climate change, terrorism, and pandemics require cooperative solutions that transcend power balancing among states.

Despite these criticisms, the Balance of Power theory remains a fundamental concept in international relations. It provides a framework for understanding why states behave as they do in an anarchic international system and how power dynamics can influence global stability. While the theory may not fully capture the complexities of modern international relations, its core principles continue to be relevant in analyzing state behavior and the pursuit of security in a competitive world.

Realism vs. Idealism in IR

Realism and Idealism are two of the most influential theories in international relations. They represent contrasting views on how the world operates and how states interact on the global stage. **Realism** is grounded in the belief that international relations are driven by the competitive pursuit of power, while **Idealism** emphasizes the potential for cooperation, ethical principles, and the importance of international institutions.

Realism is based on a pessimistic view of human nature, which assumes that individuals and states are inherently self-interested and power-seeking. Realists believe that the international system is anarchic—there is no central authority to enforce rules or protect states. In such a system, states are primarily concerned with their own survival and security. This leads to a focus on power, particularly military power, as the key to ensuring a state's safety and influence.

Realists argue that **conflict is inevitable** in international relations because states are always in competition for resources, security, and influence. This competition often results in a balance of power, where states or alliances maintain equilibrium to prevent any one state from becoming too powerful. The Balance of Power theory, which posits that stability is achieved when power is evenly distributed among states, is a central concept in Realism. Realists see the international arena as a zero-sum game, where one state's gain is often another's loss.

Prominent realists, such as **Hans Morgenthau** and **Kenneth Waltz**, have shaped the theory with their ideas. Morgenthau's "Politics Among Nations" emphasizes the role of power and the inevitability of conflict, arguing that moral principles cannot be applied to the actions of states in the same way they are to individuals. Waltz's "Theory of International Politics" introduces the concept of structural realism or neorealism, which focuses on the international system's structure rather than human nature as the driving force behind state behavior.

In contrast, **Idealism** is rooted in a more optimistic view of international relations. Idealists believe that human nature is not entirely selfish and that states can cooperate to achieve common goals. Idealism emphasizes the role of international law, moral values, and international organizations in promoting peace and cooperation. Idealists argue that **conflict can be reduced** through diplomacy, international agreements, and the establishment of global norms that encourage peaceful interactions.

Woodrow Wilson is one of the most notable Idealists in international relations. His vision of a League of Nations, proposed after World War I, was based on the idea that international cooperation and collective security could prevent future conflicts. Wilson believed that a world governed by international law and guided by moral principles could lead to lasting peace. Although the League of Nations ultimately failed to prevent World War II, Wilson's ideas laid the groundwork for the establishment of the United Nations, a key institution in global governance today.

Idealists also emphasize the importance of **human rights** and ethical considerations in international relations. They argue that states have a moral responsibility to protect the rights and well-being of individuals, not just pursue their own interests. This perspective has led to the development of international human rights norms, humanitarian interventions, and the Responsibility to Protect (R2P) doctrine, which argues that the international community should intervene when a state fails to protect its population from atrocities.

The debate between Realism and Idealism reflects the tension between power and morality in international relations. Realists criticize Idealists for being naive, arguing that Idealism overlooks the harsh realities of international politics, where power and self-interest often dominate. They contend that Idealism's focus on cooperation and morality can lead to misguided policies that ignore the fundamental nature of the international system.

On the other hand, Idealists argue that Realism is overly cynical and deterministic. They believe that Realism's focus on power and conflict perpetuates a cycle of violence and mistrust. Idealists advocate for a more constructive approach to international relations, one that seeks to build a more just and peaceful world through cooperation, dialogue, and the strengthening of international institutions.

In practice, international relations often involve a blend of both Realist and Idealist principles. States may pursue power and security, as Realism suggests, but they also engage in diplomacy, form international institutions, and adhere to global norms that align with Idealist views. The balance between these approaches depends on the specific context and the goals of the states involved.

Understanding the differences between Realism and Idealism is essential for analyzing global politics. These theories offer distinct lenses through which to view international events, and they continue to shape debates and policies in the field of international relations.

The Impact of Globalization on IR

Globalization refers to the process by which economies, societies, and cultures become increasingly interconnected and interdependent. This phenomenon has had profound effects on international relations (IR), reshaping how states interact, cooperate, and compete on the global stage. The impact of globalization on IR is multifaceted, influencing everything from economic policies and security strategies to cultural exchanges and environmental cooperation.

Economic interdependence is one of the most significant impacts of globalization on IR. As trade barriers have fallen and technology has advanced, countries are now more economically connected than ever before. Global supply chains link producers and consumers across continents, and financial markets react instantly to developments in any part of the world. This interconnectedness has led to a situation where the economic fortunes of countries are closely tied together. For example, a financial crisis in one country can quickly spread to others, as seen during the 2008 global financial crisis. This economic interdependence encourages cooperation, as states recognize that their economic well-being is linked to the stability of the global economy.

However, economic globalization also creates **new challenges and tensions**. The competition for markets, resources, and investment can lead to conflicts between states, particularly when there are disparities in economic power. Globalization has also led to concerns about economic sovereignty, as multinational corporations (MNCs) and international financial institutions exert significant influence over national policies. Countries may feel pressured to adopt economic policies that favor global markets rather than their own citizens, leading to tensions between national interests and global economic forces.

Cultural globalization has also had a profound impact on IR. The global flow of information, ideas, and cultural products has created a more interconnected world, where people are exposed to diverse cultures and perspectives. This can lead to greater understanding and cooperation between states, as cultural exchanges foster mutual respect and dialogue. However, cultural globalization can also lead to conflicts, particularly when it is perceived as a threat to local identities and traditions. The spread of Western cultural products, such as movies, music, and fashion, has sometimes been met with resistance in non-Western societies, where it is seen as a form of cultural imperialism.

Globalization has also transformed the nature of security in international relations. In the past, security was primarily understood in terms of military power and the defense of national borders. Today, however, security threats are increasingly transnational and non-military in nature. Issues such as terrorism, cyber-attacks, pandemics, and climate change do not respect national borders, requiring international cooperation to address. For instance, the global response to the COVID-19 pandemic highlighted the need for coordinated international action, as no single country could effectively combat the virus on its own.

Globalization has also led to the rise of **new actors in international relations**. While states remain the primary actors, non-state actors such as international organizations, NGOs, and MNCs have gained significant influence. These actors often operate across borders and can shape international policies and norms. For example, international organizations like the World Health Organization (WHO) are important in coordinating responses to global health crises, while NGOs like Amnesty International advocate for human rights on a global scale. The influence of these actors challenges the traditional state-centric view of international relations, as power is increasingly dispersed across multiple levels.

Environmental issues have become a key area where globalization impacts IR. As the world becomes more interconnected, the environmental challenges facing humanity—such as climate change, deforestation, and biodiversity loss—are increasingly seen as global problems requiring collective action. Global environmental agreements, like the Paris Agreement on climate change, illustrate how states are coming together to address these issues. However, achieving meaningful cooperation can be difficult, as different countries have varying levels of responsibility, capability, and willingness to take action.

Despite the many benefits of globalization, it has also led to a **backlash in some parts of the world.** Concerns about economic inequality, cultural homogenization, and loss of sovereignty have fueled nationalist and protectionist movements. These movements often advocate for policies that prioritize national interests over global cooperation, challenging the very foundations of globalization. The rise of populist leaders in countries like the United States and the United Kingdom, who have pushed for policies such as Brexit and trade protectionism, reflects this trend.

In summary, globalization has fundamentally transformed international relations, creating new opportunities for cooperation but also new challenges and conflicts. The interconnectedness of the global economy, the spread of cultural influences, the rise of new security threats, and the emergence of non-state actors have all reshaped how states interact on the global stage. As globalization evolves, so too will the dynamics of international relations, requiring states and other actors to adapt to an increasingly complex and interconnected world.

Non-State Actors: NGOs, IGOs, and Multinational Corporations

Non-state actors have become increasingly influential in international relations, complementing and sometimes challenging the traditional dominance of states. Among the most significant non-state actors are non-governmental organizations (NGOs), intergovernmental organizations (IGOs), and multinational corporations (MNCs). Each of these entities plays a unique role in shaping global policies, norms, and actions.

Non-governmental organizations (NGOs) are private, voluntary groups that work to address various global issues, such as human rights, environmental protection, and humanitarian aid. NGOs operate independently of governments, although they often collaborate with them. Their influence in international relations stems from their ability to mobilize public opinion, conduct research, and advocate for policy changes. For example, organizations like Amnesty International and Human Rights Watch have been instrumental in bringing attention to human rights abuses around the world. They often serve as watchdogs, holding governments accountable for their actions and pushing for adherence to international norms.

NGOs also are important in **humanitarian efforts**. Organizations like the International Red Cross and Médecins Sans Frontières (Doctors Without Borders) provide essential services in conflict zones, disaster areas, and impoverished regions. They can operate in places where governments may be unwilling or unable to act, offering assistance to those most in need. Through their work, NGOs often influence international policies on humanitarian aid, development, and conflict resolution.

Intergovernmental organizations (IGOs) are entities created by states to facilitate cooperation on specific issues. These organizations are composed of member states and are established by treaties or agreements. IGOs play a critical role in international relations by providing a platform for dialogue, coordination, and decision-making among states. The United Nations (UN), the World Trade Organization (WTO), and the International Monetary Fund (IMF) are prominent examples of IGOs that influence global governance.

The **United Nations** is perhaps the most significant IGO, with its various bodies addressing issues such as peace and security, human rights, and sustainable development. The UN Security Council, for instance, is responsible for maintaining international peace and security, making decisions on interventions, sanctions, and peacekeeping missions. The World Trade Organization (WTO) facilitates global trade by establishing rules and resolving disputes between member states, while the International Monetary Fund (IMF) provides financial assistance and advice to countries facing economic challenges.

IGOs are often seen as **facilitators of international cooperation**. They help states address issues that transcend national borders, such as climate change, health pandemics, and global trade. However, their effectiveness can be limited by the interests of powerful member states and the need for consensus among diverse participants. Despite these challenges, IGOs remain essential to the functioning of the international system, providing a forum for cooperation and conflict resolution.

Multinational corporations (MNCs) are another powerful non-state actor in international relations. These are large companies that operate in multiple countries, influencing global trade, investment, and economic policies. MNCs like Apple, Microsoft, and Toyota have revenues that surpass the GDPs of many countries, giving them significant economic leverage. They can shape global markets, set industry standards, and influence the policies of governments where they operate.

MNCs are often at the forefront of **globalization**, driving economic integration through their operations. They invest in different countries, create jobs, and transfer technology, contributing to economic development. However, MNCs can also be controversial figures in international relations. Their pursuit of profit can sometimes lead to negative impacts, such as labor exploitation, environmental degradation, and undermining of local industries. Additionally, MNCs often engage in **lobbying** and influence government policies to favor their business interests, which can raise concerns about their power over national sovereignty and democratic processes.

The influence of MNCs extends beyond economics. They can also impact **social and cultural dynamics** through their global reach. For example, the global presence of companies like McDonald's and Coca-Cola has contributed to the spread of Western consumer culture, affecting local customs and lifestyles. This cultural influence, often termed "McDonaldization," reflects the broader impact MNCs can have on societies around the world.

The roles of NGOs, IGOs, and MNCs highlight the increasing complexity of international relations in the modern world. **These non-state actors** complement the actions of states, often filling gaps in areas where states may be ineffective or unwilling to act. They bring new perspectives, resources, and methods to address global challenges, from human rights and environmental protection to economic development and conflict resolution.

However, the rise of non-state actors also raises questions about accountability and legitimacy in international relations. Unlike states, which are accountable to their citizens, NGOs, IGOs, and MNCs operate on a different level, often with less direct oversight. This can lead to tensions between their global influence and the need for transparency and accountability in their actions.

The Evolution of International Relations as a Discipline

International Relations as a discipline has evolved significantly since its inception, driven by historical events, theoretical developments, and the changing dynamics of global politics. The study of IR has grown from a focus on diplomacy and war to encompass a wide range of issues, including economics, culture, human rights, and the environment. This evolution reflects the complexity of the international system and the diverse factors that influence global interactions.

The roots of IR can be traced back to the aftermath of World War I, when the need to understand and prevent future conflicts became a priority for scholars and policymakers. The devastation of the war highlighted the limitations of traditional diplomacy and the need for a systematic study of international affairs. In 1919, the first academic chair in IR was established at the University of Wales, Aberystwyth, marking the formal beginning of the discipline. The early focus of IR was on understanding the causes of war and developing strategies for peace, with a strong emphasis on diplomacy, international law, and the balance of power.

Realism emerged as the dominant theoretical framework in the early years of IR. Influenced by the works of political thinkers like Thomas Hobbes and Niccolò Machiavelli, realism viewed international relations as a struggle for power among self-interested states in an anarchic system. Realists argued that states must prioritize their security and power to survive in a world where there is no overarching authority to enforce rules or protect them. The interwar period and the outbreak of World War II reinforced the realist perspective, as the failure of the League of Nations and the rise of aggressive states like Nazi Germany demonstrated the limitations of idealistic approaches to peace.

After World War II, the discipline of IR expanded both in scope and theoretical diversity. The establishment of the United Nations and the beginning of the Cold War introduced new challenges and opportunities for IR scholars. The bipolar world order, dominated by the United States and the Soviet Union, led to the development of new theories and approaches to understanding international relations. Liberalism, for example, emerged as a counterpoint to realism, emphasizing the potential for cooperation among states through international institutions, trade, and the spread of democracy. The European integration process, particularly the formation of the European Union, provided a real-world example of liberalism in action.

The Cold War also spurred the development of strategic studies and nuclear deterrence theory, which became central concerns for IR scholars. The concept of mutually assured destruction (MAD) and the delicate balance of power between the superpowers required a deep understanding of military strategy, arms control, and crisis management. The study of IR during this period was heavily influenced by the need to prevent nuclear war and manage the global rivalry between the East and the West.

In the post-Cold War era, IR as a discipline has continued to evolve in response to global changes. The collapse of the Soviet Union and the emergence of the United States as the sole superpower led to new questions about the nature of power and order in a unipolar world. At the same time, the rise of globalization, the spread of democracy, and the increasing importance of non-state actors, such as multinational corporations and international organizations, have broadened the focus of IR. Issues like human rights, environmental sustainability, and global governance have become central to the study of international relations, reflecting the interconnectedness of the modern world.

Theoretical diversity has also increased in the field of IR. Constructivism, for example, emerged in the 1990s as a significant approach, challenging the materialist focus of realism and liberalism. Constructivists argue that international relations are shaped by social structures, ideas, and identities, rather than just material power. This perspective has opened up new avenues for understanding how norms, values, and beliefs influence state behavior and the international system.

Critical theories, such as Marxism, feminism, and postcolonialism, have also gained prominence in IR. These approaches challenge the traditional state-centric and power-oriented focus of the discipline, instead highlighting issues of inequality, exploitation, and the voices of marginalized groups. Feminist IR scholars, for instance, have brought attention to the role of gender in global politics, while postcolonial theorists have explored the legacies of colonialism and the impact of imperialism on contemporary international relations.

The study of IR has also become more interdisciplinary, drawing on insights from economics, sociology, history, law, and environmental studies. This interdisciplinary approach reflects the complexity of global issues, which cannot be fully understood through the lens of a single discipline. For example, the study of global environmental governance requires an understanding of both international law and ecological science, while the analysis of global financial crises involves economics, political science, and international relations.

Methodologically, IR has also seen significant developments. The field has embraced both qualitative and quantitative research methods, including case studies, statistical analysis, and formal modeling. This methodological pluralism has allowed IR scholars to tackle a wide range of research questions and provide more nuanced and empirically grounded insights into international phenomena.

CHAPTER 2: THEORIES OF INTERNATIONAL RELATIONS

Realism and Neorealism

Realism is one of the oldest and most influential theories in international relations. It is grounded in a view of human nature that sees individuals as inherently self-interested and power-seeking. This perspective extends to states, which are seen as the primary actors in an anarchic international system where no central authority exists to enforce rules or norms. **In this environment, states prioritize their survival and security**, often competing with one another for power and resources.

At the heart of realism is the concept of power, particularly military power. Realists argue that states must be vigilant and prepared to defend themselves, as the international system is inherently competitive and conflict-prone. They view international relations as a zero-sum game, where the gain of one state often comes at the expense of another. This leads to a focus on balance of power, a key idea in realism that suggests stability in the international system can be maintained when power is distributed among several states in such a way that no single state or coalition dominates.

Realism emphasizes the role of national interest in guiding state behavior. States are driven by the need to secure their own interests, which are often defined in terms of power, security, and survival. **Moral considerations, while not entirely dismissed, are secondary to the pragmatic concerns of maintaining power and ensuring state survival.** For realists, international law and institutions are limited in their ability to constrain state behavior because they lack enforcement mechanisms and are often overridden by the strategic interests of powerful states.

Hans Morgenthau is one of the most prominent figures associated with classical realism. In his seminal work, *Politics Among Nations*, Morgenthau argues that politics, like society in general, is governed by objective laws rooted in human nature. He asserts that the drive for power is a fundamental aspect of human behavior, and this drive translates into the actions of states in the international arena. Morgenthau's realism is often referred to as classical realism because it emphasizes the influence of human nature on state behavior.

Neorealism, also known as structural realism, emerged in the 20th century as a refinement of classical realism. Kenneth Waltz, a key figure in the development of neorealism, shifted the focus from human nature to the structure of the international system itself. In his influential book, *Theory of International Politics*, Waltz argues that the anarchic structure of the international system compels states to act in certain ways, regardless of their internal characteristics or the personalities of their leaders.

For neorealists, the distribution of power within the international system is the primary factor that determines state behavior. **Waltz introduces the concept of polarity—unipolar, bipolar, and multipolar systems—to explain how the structure of power affects the likelihood of conflict or stability.** In a bipolar system, for example, power is concentrated in two dominant states or blocs, which can lead to stability because both sides are deterred by the other's strength. The Cold War is often cited as an example of a bipolar system that, despite intense rivalry, maintained a degree of stability due to the balance of power between the United States and the Soviet Union.

Neorealism also introduces the idea of defensive and offensive realism. **Defensive realists, like Waltz, believe that states are primarily concerned with maintaining their security rather than expanding their power.** They argue that aggressive expansion can provoke counterbalancing efforts by other states, leading to a security dilemma where the pursuit of more power actually makes a state less secure. On the other hand, offensive realists, such as John Mearsheimer, argue that the anarchic nature of the international system compels states to seek maximum power to ensure their survival. In this view, power maximization is the best strategy for security in an uncertain and competitive world.

While realism and neorealism share many core assumptions, such as the importance of the state and the anarchic nature of the international system, they differ in their explanations of state behavior. **Classical realism focuses on human nature and the role of individual statesmen in shaping foreign policy.** In contrast, neorealism emphasizes the structural constraints imposed by the international system, suggesting that the behavior of states is largely determined by their relative power within this system.

Both realism and neorealism have been influential in shaping the study of international relations. They offer a lens through which to view global politics that emphasizes the enduring role of power, competition, and the challenges posed by an anarchic international system.

Liberalism and Neoliberalism

Liberalism in international relations is a theory that contrasts sharply with realism. Where realism views the international system as inherently conflictual and driven by power politics, liberalism offers a more optimistic perspective. It emphasizes the potential for cooperation, the importance of international institutions, and the role of economic interdependence in promoting peace.

At its core, liberalism argues that human nature is not solely self-interested and power-seeking. Instead, it posits that individuals and, by extension, states can cooperate for mutual benefit. Liberal thinkers believe that states are capable of transcending the anarchic structure of the international system through collaboration, shared values, and institutions. The roots of liberalism in international relations can be traced back to the Enlightenment, with thinkers like Immanuel Kant, who argued that republics—states governed by the rule of law—are more likely to cooperate and avoid war.

One of the key tenets of liberalism is the idea that **democratic states are less likely to go to war with one another**. This idea, known as the Democratic Peace Theory, suggests that democracies have a unique internal structure that fosters peaceful international relations. Democracies are believed to be more transparent, accountable to their citizens, and inclined to resolve conflicts through negotiation rather than force. This theory has been supported by empirical research showing that democratic states rarely, if ever, engage in wars with each other, though they may still go to war with non-democratic states.

Economic interdependence is another central concept in liberalism. Liberal theorists argue that when states are economically interconnected, the costs of conflict increase, making war less attractive. Trade, investment, and economic cooperation create mutual dependencies that bind states together, reducing the likelihood of conflict. For example, the European Union (EU) is often cited as a successful case where economic integration has helped maintain peace in a region historically plagued by wars.

International institutions are also crucial in liberalism. These institutions, such as the United Nations, the World Trade Organization (WTO), and the International Monetary Fund (IMF), are seen as mechanisms that facilitate cooperation, resolve disputes, and promote global governance. Liberals argue that these institutions help mitigate the effects of anarchy by providing a framework for cooperation and collective action. They create rules, norms, and procedures that states can rely on to manage conflicts and achieve common goals.

Neoliberalism is a modern adaptation of classical liberalism that emerged in response to the dominance of realism, particularly during the Cold War. While it shares many principles with classical liberalism, neoliberalism is more focused on the role of institutions in fostering cooperation in an anarchic international system. Neoliberals accept some of the realist assumptions, such as the importance of the state and the challenges posed by anarchy, but they argue that these challenges can be managed through institutional arrangements.

Robert Keohane is one of the most prominent figures associated with neoliberalism. In his influential book *After Hegemony*, Keohane argues that even in the absence of a dominant power (or hegemon), states can cooperate through institutions. He challenges the realist notion that cooperation is only possible when there is a clear power hierarchy. Instead, Keohane suggests that international institutions provide the rules and norms that facilitate cooperation by reducing uncertainty, lowering transaction costs, and making state behavior more predictable.

Neoliberalism also emphasizes the importance of **complex interdependence**, a concept developed by Keohane and Joseph Nye. Complex interdependence refers to the multiple, overlapping connections between states, including economic, political, and social ties. This interdependence creates a situation where states have multiple interests in maintaining peaceful relations and are less likely to resort to conflict. Neoliberalism argues that in a world of complex interdependence, the use of military force becomes less effective as a tool of statecraft, while diplomacy, economic cooperation, and multilateralism gain importance.

However, **neoliberalism is not without its critics**. Some argue that it underestimates the persistence of power politics and the influence of nationalism and identity in international relations. Critics also suggest that neoliberalism may be overly optimistic about the capacity of institutions to manage conflicts, particularly in cases where powerful states choose to ignore or undermine these institutions. The Iraq War in 2003, where the United States led an invasion with limited international support, is often cited as an example of the limitations of neoliberalism in restraining unilateral action by powerful states.

Despite these criticisms, **liberalism and neoliberalism remain influential theories** in international relations. They offer a framework for understanding how cooperation can be achieved in a competitive international system and highlight the importance of democracy, economic interdependence, and international institutions in promoting global stability. As globalization continues to deepen connections between states, the relevance of liberal and neoliberal ideas in shaping international relations is likely to persist.

Constructivism in International Relations

Constructivism is a relatively recent but highly influential theory in international relations. Unlike realism and liberalism, which focus on material factors like power and institutions, constructivism emphasizes the role of ideas, identities, and norms in shaping international relations. **Constructivists argue that the international system is not a fixed structure but is socially constructed through the interactions and beliefs of states and other actors.**

The central premise of constructivism is that **ideas and beliefs shape how states perceive and interact with each other**. According to constructivists, the international system is not simply an anarchic environment where states compete for power, as realists argue, but a social structure where meaning and behavior are created through social interaction. For example, the concept of sovereignty is not a natural or inevitable feature of international relations; it is a social construct that has evolved over time through the shared understanding and practices of states.

Identity is a key concept in constructivism. Constructivists argue that the identities of states—how they see themselves and others—are important in shaping their foreign policies and interactions. These identities are not fixed; they can change over time based on experiences, relationships, and internal or external influences. For instance, Germany's identity as a peaceful, cooperative state in the post-World War II era contrasts sharply with its identity as a militaristic power before and during the war. This shift in identity has influenced Germany's foreign policy, particularly its strong commitment to European integration and multilateralism.

Norms, or shared expectations about appropriate behavior, are another central focus of constructivism. Norms influence how states behave and how they are perceived by others. For example, the norm against the use of chemical weapons has been so deeply ingrained in international society that states using such weapons face severe condemnation and potential retaliation from the international community. These norms are not just rules imposed from above; they are maintained and reinforced through the actions and beliefs of states and other actors.

Constructivism also highlights the importance of discourse and language in international relations. The way states talk about issues, frame conflicts, and describe their relationships with others can shape perceptions and outcomes. For instance, the framing of the "war on terror" after the September 11 attacks shaped global responses to terrorism and influenced the policies of many states. Constructivists study how language and discourse create and reinforce identities, norms, and power dynamics in the international system.

Alexander Wendt is one of the most prominent constructivist theorists. In his seminal work *Social Theory of International Politics*, Wendt argues that "anarchy is what states make of it." This means that the anarchic structure of the international system does not inherently lead to conflict or cooperation; rather, the outcomes depend on how states perceive and interact with each other. If states view each other as enemies, anarchy will lead to competition and conflict. However, if they see each other as friends or partners, anarchy can foster cooperation and peace.

Constructivism challenges the deterministic views of realism and liberalism by emphasizing the agency of states and other actors in shaping the international system. While realists see the international system as a rigid structure that forces states to act in certain ways, constructivists argue that states have the power to change the system through their actions, beliefs, and interactions. This perspective opens up possibilities for change and transformation in international relations, as it suggests that global norms and identities can evolve over time.

One of the strengths of constructivism is its ability to explain changes in international norms and practices. For example, the global movement toward human rights and humanitarian intervention can be understood through a

24

constructivist lens. As norms around human rights have strengthened, states have increasingly accepted the idea that they have a responsibility to protect populations from atrocities, even if it means intervening in another state's affairs. This shift reflects a change in the collective understanding of state sovereignty and human rights, driven by advocacy, discourse, and changing identities.

However, constructivism also faces criticisms. Some argue that it is too focused on ideas and norms, neglecting the material realities of power and economics that also shape international relations. Critics also suggest that constructivism can be difficult to apply in practice, as it relies heavily on the interpretation of social and historical contexts, which can be subjective and complex.

Despite these critiques, **constructivism has made significant contributions to the study of international relations.** It offers a nuanced understanding of how the international system is shaped by the beliefs, identities, and interactions of its actors.

Marxism and Critical Theories

Marxism in international relations offers a fundamentally different lens from traditional theories like realism and liberalism. It is rooted in the ideas of Karl Marx, who focused on the role of economic structures, class struggle, and the exploitation inherent in capitalism. **Marxist theory in IR** views the global system as a hierarchy, where the wealthy, capitalist states (often referred to as the "core") exploit poorer, less developed states (the "periphery"). This perspective highlights the unequal distribution of power and wealth on a global scale, driven by the dynamics of capitalism.

At the heart of Marxist theory in international relations is the concept of imperialism. According to Marxists, imperialism is the highest stage of capitalism, where powerful states extend their influence and control over weaker regions to exploit their resources, labor, and markets. This process is not just economic but also political and cultural, as dominant states impose their systems and ideologies on subordinate states. The economic relationships established under imperialism create a global division of labor, where the periphery provides raw materials and cheap labor, while the core produces high-value goods and services. This division reinforces the dependency of the periphery on the core, perpetuating inequality and underdevelopment.

Dependency theory emerged as a key offshoot of Marxist thought in international relations. It argues that the economic development of the periphery is systematically constrained by its dependency on the core. Dependency theorists like André Gunder Frank and Immanuel Wallerstein argue that the global capitalist system is designed to benefit the core at the expense of the periphery. This dependency is maintained through unequal trade relations, debt, and the influence of multinational corporations and international financial institutions like the IMF and World Bank. As a result, the periphery remains trapped in a cycle of poverty and underdevelopment, unable to achieve meaningful economic growth or autonomy.

Critical theory in international relations, while influenced by Marxism, expands the scope of analysis beyond economic structures to include issues of culture, ideology, and power in a broader sense. Critical theorists, drawing on the work of scholars like Antonio Gramsci and the Frankfurt School, argue that the dominant ideas and norms in global politics serve to perpetuate existing power structures. They are interested in how consent for these power structures is manufactured and maintained through cultural institutions, media, and education. **Gramsci's concept of hegemony** is central to this analysis, as it explains how the ruling class maintains control not just through force, but by shaping the beliefs and values of society to align with their interests.

One of the key contributions of critical theory is its focus on emancipation. Critical theorists are concerned with uncovering the ways in which power structures oppress and exploit individuals and groups, with the ultimate goal of achieving social justice and liberation. In international relations, this involves challenging the dominant paradigms that justify inequality, war, and exploitation. Critical theorists advocate for a more just and equitable world order, where power is distributed more fairly and the voices of marginalized and oppressed groups are heard.

Postcolonial theory is a critical approach that examines the lingering effects of colonialism on international relations. Postcolonial scholars argue that the legacy of colonialism continues to shape global power dynamics, particularly in the way the Global South interacts with the Global North. They explore how colonial histories influence contemporary issues such as race, identity, and development. Postcolonial theory challenges the Eurocentric narratives that dominate IR, calling for a more inclusive understanding of global politics that recognizes the experiences and perspectives of formerly colonized peoples.

Feminist theory is another important strand of critical theory in international relations. Feminist theorists argue that traditional IR theories have been dominated by male perspectives, which often overlook or marginalize the experiences and contributions of women. Feminist IR scholars seek to highlight how gender shapes global politics, from the way wars are fought to the formulation of foreign policy. They argue that issues such as sexual violence in conflict, the gendered division of labor, and the role of women in peacebuilding have been neglected in mainstream IR theory.

Marxism and critical theories challenge the status quo in international relations by focusing on the underlying power structures and inequalities that shape global politics. They offer a critique of traditional IR theories, which they argue are complicit in maintaining a system that benefits the powerful at the expense of the marginalized. By emphasizing the role of economic exploitation, cultural hegemony, and social justice, these theories provide a framework for understanding and addressing the deep-rooted inequalities in the international system.

Feminist Theories in International Relations

Feminist theories in international relations bring a critical perspective to the study of global politics, challenging the traditional, male-dominated frameworks that have historically shaped the field. **Feminist IR scholars argue that gender is a fundamental aspect of international relations**, influencing everything from the conduct of war to the formulation of foreign policy. They seek to uncover how global politics affects men and women differently and to highlight the ways in which traditional IR theories have marginalized or ignored the experiences and contributions of women.

One of the central tenets of feminist IR theory is the concept of gendered power relations. Feminists argue that the international system is deeply gendered, with power and authority typically associated with masculine traits such as aggression, competition, and rationality. In contrast, traits traditionally associated with femininity, such as empathy, cooperation, and care, are often undervalued or dismissed. This gendered understanding of power affects how states interact, how conflicts are managed, and how global issues are prioritized.

Feminist IR theory also emphasizes the **importance of including women's experiences** in the analysis of international relations. Traditional IR has often overlooked the impact of global politics on women, particularly in areas like conflict, peacebuilding, and development. Feminists highlight how women are disproportionately affected by war, often experiencing violence, displacement, and loss of livelihood. They also point out that women are frequently excluded from peace negotiations and decision-making processes, despite their significant roles in grassroots peacebuilding efforts.

Intersectionality is a key concept in feminist IR theory. Intersectionality recognizes that gender does not operate in isolation but is interconnected with other forms of identity and oppression, such as race, class, and nationality. Feminist IR scholars use intersectionality to examine how these different identities and power structures intersect to shape the experiences of individuals and groups in the international system. For example, women of color or women in the Global South may face unique challenges that differ from those experienced by women in more privileged positions.

Feminist IR theory also critiques the traditional focus on state-centric, militarized approaches to security. Feminists argue for a broader understanding of security that includes human security—focusing on the protection and well-being of individuals rather than just the defense of state borders. **This perspective shifts the focus from military power to issues like economic security, access to healthcare, and protection from violence**, arguing that true security cannot be achieved without addressing these fundamental human needs.

Finally, feminist IR theory calls for the inclusion of women in decision-making processes at all levels of international relations. Feminists argue that greater gender equality in leadership positions can lead to more just and equitable policies, particularly in areas like conflict resolution, development, and human rights. The push for initiatives such as UN Security Council Resolution 1325, which calls for the increased participation of women in peace and security efforts, reflects the influence of feminist ideas in international relations.

Feminist theories in international relations challenge the traditional assumptions and biases of the field, advocating for a more inclusive and equitable approach to understanding global politics.

CHAPTER 3: GLOBAL GOVERNANCE AND INSTITUTIONS

The United Nations and its Role

The United Nations (UN) is one of the most significant international organizations in the world, established with the primary goal of maintaining international peace and security. Founded in 1945, after the devastation of World War II, the UN was created to prevent such a conflict from happening again. **Today, the UN has a central role in global governance**, addressing a wide range of issues from conflict resolution to human rights, development, and climate change.

The UN's structure is designed to manage a variety of global challenges. It is composed of several key bodies, each with specific responsibilities. The General Assembly is the main deliberative body where all 193 member states have equal representation. It serves as a forum for discussing and addressing international issues, from security to health and the environment. While the General Assembly's resolutions are non-binding, they carry significant moral and political weight, reflecting the consensus or concerns of the international community.

The **Security Council** is perhaps the most powerful body within the UN. It is responsible for maintaining international peace and security, and it has the authority to make binding decisions that member states are obligated to implement. The Security Council can impose sanctions, authorize the use of force, and establish peacekeeping missions. It is composed of 15 members: five permanent members—China, France, Russia, the United Kingdom, and the United States—who have veto power, and ten non-permanent members elected for two-year terms. The veto power of the permanent members is a significant aspect of the Security Council's operations, as it allows any one of these states to block resolutions, often leading to criticism that the Security Council can be paralyzed by the interests of its most powerful members.

Peacekeeping is one of the most visible roles of the UN. UN peacekeepers, often called Blue Helmets, are deployed to conflict zones around the world to help maintain ceasefires, protect civilians, and support the implementation of peace agreements. These missions are authorized by the Security Council and are carried out by troops and police from member states. While peacekeeping missions have had successes, such as in Namibia and El Salvador, they have also faced challenges, including allegations of misconduct and failures to protect civilians, as seen in Rwanda and Bosnia.

Human rights protection is another critical aspect of the UN's work. The UN's commitment to human rights is enshrined in the Universal Declaration of Human Rights, adopted by the General Assembly in 1948. This document sets out fundamental rights and freedoms that all people are entitled to, regardless of nationality, gender, race, or religion. The UN Human Rights Council, a subsidiary body of the General Assembly, monitors human rights violations and works to promote and protect these rights worldwide. However, the effectiveness of the Human Rights Council has been questioned due to the inclusion of member states with poor human rights records, which can undermine its credibility and actions.

The UN also is important in development and humanitarian assistance. Through agencies like the United Nations Development Programme (UNDP), the World Food Programme (WFP), and the United Nations Children's Fund (UNICEF), the UN works to reduce poverty, promote education, improve health, and provide emergency assistance in crises. The UN's Sustainable Development Goals (SDGs), adopted in 2015, set out an ambitious agenda to end poverty, protect the planet, and ensure prosperity for all by 2030. These goals reflect the UN's broad commitment to addressing the root causes of conflict and inequality through development.

In the area of climate change, the UN has been instrumental in facilitating international agreements. The UN Framework Convention on Climate Change (UNFCCC) and its subsequent agreements, such as the Kyoto Protocol and the Paris Agreement, provide the foundation for global efforts to combat climate change. The Paris Agreement, adopted in 2015, is particularly notable as it brought together nearly every country in the world to commit to limiting global warming and reducing greenhouse gas emissions. The UN's role in this process demonstrates its capacity to bring states together to address global challenges that no single country can solve alone.

The UN's role in global health has also been significant, particularly through the World Health Organization (WHO). The WHO coordinates international responses to health crises, such as the COVID-19 pandemic, and works to combat diseases, promote health, and ensure access to medical services worldwide. The UN's efforts in global health illustrate its broader mission to improve the well-being of people around the world, addressing issues that cross borders and require collective action.

However, the UN isn't without its challenges. **The organization often faces criticism for its bureaucracy, inefficiency, and the influence of powerful states on its decision-making processes.** The structure of the Security Council, with its permanent members and veto power, is frequently cited as a significant barrier to effective action, particularly when the interests of these powerful states are at odds. Additionally, funding constraints and political pressures can limit the UN's ability to carry out its missions and achieve its goals.

Despite these challenges, the UN remains a central actor in global governance. Its ability to convene states, facilitate dialogue, and coordinate collective action on a wide range of issues makes it an indispensable part of the international system.

The UN's role in promoting peace, protecting human rights, fostering development, and addressing global challenges like climate change underscores its enduring relevance in a complex and interconnected world.

International Law and Treaties

International law is a critical component of global governance, providing a framework for the interactions between states and other international actors. Unlike domestic law, which is enforced by a centralized authority within a state, international law operates in an anarchic system where there is no overarching government. Despite this, international law plays a vital role in regulating state behavior, resolving disputes, and promoting peace, security, and cooperation.

International law is primarily made through treaties and customary international law. Treaties are formal agreements between states that are legally binding. They can cover a wide range of issues, including trade, human rights, environmental protection, and arms control. When states sign and ratify a treaty, they commit to adhering to its provisions. For example, the United Nations Charter, a foundational treaty, outlines the principles of international peace and security, the roles of the UN's main bodies, and the rights and duties of member states.

Customary international law emerges from the consistent practice of states, coupled with the belief that such practices are legally required, known as opinio juris. Over time, certain practices become accepted as binding legal norms, even without formal agreements. For instance, the prohibition against genocide and the principle of diplomatic immunity are widely recognized as customary international law, binding on all states regardless of whether they have signed specific treaties on these issues.

The development of international law has been significantly shaped by historical events. After the devastation of World War II, there was a strong push to create a legal framework to prevent future conflicts and promote international cooperation. This led to the establishment of key institutions and treaties, such as the United Nations, the International Court of Justice (ICJ), and the Universal Declaration of Human Rights. The Nuremberg Trials, where Nazi war criminals were prosecuted, also set important precedents for international criminal law, affirming that individuals, not just states, could be held accountable for violations of international law.

The International Court of Justice (ICJ), often referred to as the World Court, is the principal judicial organ of the United Nations. It settles disputes between states and gives advisory opinions on legal questions referred to it by the UN General Assembly, Security Council, or other authorized bodies. While the ICJ's rulings are binding, its jurisdiction is based on the consent of the states involved, which means that states must agree to submit to the court's authority. This can limit the effectiveness of the ICJ, as powerful states may choose not to participate or comply with its decisions.

Human rights law is a significant area of international law, with numerous treaties and conventions dedicated to protecting individuals from abuses. The Universal Declaration of Human Rights, adopted by the UN General Assembly in 1948, is a milestone document that outlines fundamental human rights to be universally protected. While the declaration itself is not legally binding, it has inspired a range of binding treaties, such as the International Covenant on Civil and Political Rights (ICCPR) and the International Covenant on Economic, Social, and Cultural Rights (ICESCR), which together with the declaration form the International Bill of Human Rights.

Environmental law is another critical area of international law that has gained prominence in recent decades. As environmental issues like climate change, biodiversity loss, and pollution transcend national borders, international cooperation is essential. Treaties like the Paris Agreement on climate change and the Convention on Biological Diversity set out commitments for states to protect the environment and promote sustainable development. These treaties reflect the growing recognition that global environmental challenges require collective action and adherence to shared legal frameworks.

International law also plays a key role in regulating the use of force and maintaining peace and security. The UN Charter is particularly important in this regard, as it prohibits the use of force by states except in cases of self-defense or when authorized by the UN Security Council. This legal framework is designed to prevent wars and conflicts, although its effectiveness depends on the willingness of states to comply and the ability of the Security Council to enforce its decisions. The Responsibility to Protect (R2P) doctrine, developed in the early 2000s, is an example of how international law is evolving to address new challenges. R2P asserts that the international community has a duty to intervene, including through military means if necessary, to prevent mass atrocities such as genocide, war crimes, ethnic cleansing, and crimes against humanity.

The enforcement of international law remains a complex and contentious issue. Unlike domestic legal systems, where courts have the authority to enforce laws, the international legal system lacks a central enforcement mechanism. Compliance with international law often relies on reciprocity, reputational concerns, and the pressure of international public opinion. In some cases, international organizations, such as the UN or regional bodies like the European Union, can impose sanctions or take collective action against states that violate international law. However, enforcement is often uneven, and powerful states may evade accountability due to their influence and strategic importance.

International law is also shaped by non-state actors, including international organizations, NGOs, and multinational corporations. These actors contribute to the development of legal norms, participate in treaty negotiations, and advocate for the enforcement of international law. For example, NGOs like Amnesty International and Human Rights Watch are important in monitoring compliance with human rights treaties and bringing attention to violations.

Treaties remain the cornerstone of international law, providing a formal mechanism for states to agree on common rules and obligations. Some treaties, like the Geneva Conventions, which regulate the conduct of armed conflict, have near-universal acceptance and are considered part of customary international law. Others, such as trade agreements or arms control treaties, are more specific and may involve only a subset of states. Treaties are typically negotiated by diplomats, signed by heads of state or government, and then ratified by the relevant legislative bodies in each participating country. Once ratified, treaties become legally binding on the states that have agreed to them, and their implementation is monitored by various international bodies.

In short, international law and treaties form the backbone of global governance, providing a framework for cooperation, conflict resolution, and the protection of human rights and the environment. While the enforcement of international law remains a challenge, the continued development of legal norms and the commitment of states and other actors to uphold these norms are essential for maintaining order and promoting justice in the international system.

Global Economic Institutions (IMF, World Bank, WTO)

Global economic institutions have a critical role in shaping the world economy, facilitating international trade, providing financial stability, and promoting development. Among the most influential of these institutions are the International Monetary Fund (IMF), the World Bank, and the World Trade Organization (WTO). **Each of these institutions has a distinct mandate, but they all contribute to the broader goal of managing and stabilizing the global economy.**

The International Monetary Fund (IMF) was established in 1944 at the Bretton Woods Conference, alongside the World Bank. The IMF's primary purpose is to ensure the stability of the international monetary system, which includes overseeing exchange rates, facilitating international trade, and providing financial assistance to countries facing balance of payments problems. **The IMF's role in global economic governance is critical,** particularly during financial crises, when it provides loans to countries in need, often in exchange for implementing specific economic reforms.

One of the key functions of the IMF is surveillance. The IMF monitors the economic and financial policies of its member countries, providing analysis and advice aimed at maintaining economic stability. This surveillance role is intended to identify potential risks to the global economy early on, allowing for preventive measures to be taken. The IMF's reports and assessments are highly influential, as they shape the economic policies of member countries and inform international investors and markets.

When countries face severe financial difficulties, the IMF can provide financial assistance through its lending programs. These loans are often conditional on the implementation of economic reforms, such as fiscal austerity, structural adjustments, or monetary policy changes. **While these programs can help stabilize economies and restore growth, they have also been criticized for imposing harsh conditions that can lead to social unrest and increased inequality.** The debate over the IMF's role in promoting austerity measures, particularly in developing countries, remains a contentious issue in global economic governance.

The World Bank, also established at the Bretton Woods Conference, focuses on long-term economic development and poverty reduction. Unlike the IMF, which primarily deals with short-term financial stability, the World Bank provides funding for development projects, such as infrastructure, education, health, and agriculture. **The World Bank's mission is to promote sustainable development and reduce poverty**, particularly in low-income countries. It provides low-interest loans, grants, and technical assistance to support development projects that can drive economic growth and improve living standards.

The World Bank's work is organized into two main institutions: the International Bank for Reconstruction and Development (IBRD), which lends to middle-income and creditworthy low-income countries, and the International Development Association (IDA), which provides concessional loans and grants to the world's poorest countries. **Through these institutions, the World Bank aims to address the root causes of poverty** and promote inclusive growth by investing in critical areas like education, healthcare, and infrastructure.

However, like the IMF, the World Bank has faced criticism for its policies and practices. Critics argue that some of the Bank's projects have led to environmental degradation, displacement of communities, and increased inequality. There are also concerns about the conditionalities attached to World Bank loans, which can impose Western-style economic models on developing countries, sometimes with mixed results. **Despite these criticisms, the World Bank remains a key player in global development**, providing essential resources and expertise to countries in need.

The World Trade Organization (WTO) is another cornerstone of the global economic system, responsible for regulating international trade. Established in 1995 as the successor to the General Agreement on Tariffs and Trade (GATT), the WTO provides a framework for negotiating trade agreements and resolving disputes between its member states. **The WTO's primary goal is to promote free and fair trade** by reducing barriers to trade, such as tariffs, subsidies, and quotas, and ensuring that trade flows as smoothly and predictably as possible.

The WTO operates on the principles of non-discrimination, reciprocity, and transparency. The principle of non-discrimination means that countries cannot discriminate between their trading partners; for example, if a country grants a trade advantage to one member, it must extend the same advantage to all other WTO members. Reciprocity involves mutual concessions in trade negotiations, where countries agree to lower their trade barriers in exchange for similar actions by others. Transparency requires countries to publish their trade policies and practices, ensuring that other members are informed and can hold each other accountable.

One of the WTO's most important functions is its dispute settlement mechanism. When trade disputes arise between member countries, the WTO provides a legal framework for resolving these disputes through a panel of experts. This mechanism is crucial for maintaining the rules-based international trading system, as it ensures that trade disagreements are settled through legal means rather than unilateral actions, which could lead to trade wars.

However, the WTO has faced significant challenges in recent years. **Negotiations under the Doha Development Round, aimed at addressing issues related to agriculture, services, and intellectual property, have stalled for over a decade, leading to questions about the organization's effectiveness in advancing global trade liberalization.** Additionally, the rise of protectionism and trade tensions, particularly between major economies like the United States and China, has further complicated the WTO's ability to fulfill its mandate. Despite these challenges, the WTO remains a central institution in global economic governance, with its rules and dispute settlement processes forming the backbone of the international trading system.

In sum, the IMF, World Bank, and WTO are key pillars of the global economic system, each with distinct but complementary roles. The IMF focuses on financial stability, the World Bank on development, and the WTO on trade. Together, they contribute to the management and stability of the global economy, although their policies and actions are often the subject of debate and criticism. As the global economy continues to evolve, these institutions will play crucial roles in addressing emerging challenges and ensuring that economic growth is sustainable and inclusive.

Regional Organizations (EU, ASEAN, African Union)

Regional organizations are vital in international relations by fostering cooperation among neighboring states, addressing regional challenges, and promoting economic integration and political stability. Among the most influential regional organizations are the European Union (EU), the Association of Southeast Asian Nations (ASEAN), and the African Union (AU). **Each of these organizations has developed its own structure, goals, and areas of focus**, reflecting the unique needs and aspirations of its member states.

The European Union (EU) is one of the most advanced examples of regional integration in the world. Originating from the European Economic Community (EEC) established by the Treaty of Rome in 1957, the EU has evolved into a supranational entity with significant authority over its member states. The EU's primary goals are to promote economic integration, ensure peace and stability in Europe, and advance democratic values.

One of the EU's most significant achievements is the creation of a single market. This allows for the free movement of goods, services, capital, and people across member states, effectively removing barriers to trade and fostering economic growth. The introduction of a common currency, the euro, in 1999 further deepened economic integration among the 19 EU member states that have adopted it. However, the EU's influence extends beyond economics. It has also developed a common foreign and security policy, allowing member states to coordinate their positions on international issues and undertake joint actions, such as peacekeeping missions.

The EU's institutional structure is complex, reflecting its unique nature as a supranational organization. The European Commission acts as the executive branch, proposing legislation and implementing decisions. The European Parliament, elected by EU citizens, shares legislative power with the Council of the European Union, which represents member states. The European Council, composed of the heads of state or government, sets the EU's overall direction. This structure allows the EU to function as a unified entity while respecting the sovereignty of its member states.

Despite its successes, the EU faces significant challenges. **The eurozone crisis, the rise of Euroscepticism, and the Brexit referendum**—where the United Kingdom voted to leave the EU—have all tested the union's cohesion. Additionally, the EU struggles with issues such as migration, climate change, and the balance of power between its institutions and member states. Nevertheless, the EU remains a powerful actor in global politics, particularly in areas like trade, climate policy, and human rights.

The Association of Southeast Asian Nations (ASEAN) was established in 1967 with the goal of promoting regional stability and economic cooperation among its ten member states in Southeast Asia. Unlike the EU, ASEAN operates on the principle of non-interference in the internal affairs of its members, emphasizing consensus-based decision-making. **This approach reflects the diverse political systems and cultures within ASEAN**, ranging from democracies to authoritarian regimes.

ASEAN's primary focus has been on economic integration and regional stability. **The ASEAN Free Trade Area (AFTA), established in the 1990s, aims to reduce tariffs and promote trade among member states.** ASEAN has also pursued deeper economic integration through initiatives like the ASEAN Economic Community (AEC), which seeks to create a single market and production base. However, economic integration within ASEAN has been less comprehensive than in the EU, partly due to the significant economic disparities among its members.

In addition to economic cooperation, ASEAN has also been important in promoting peace and security in the region. The organization has been instrumental in addressing regional conflicts, such as the Cambodian-Vietnamese war and the South China Sea disputes. ASEAN's diplomatic efforts, often conducted through the ASEAN Regional Forum (ARF), have helped to manage tensions and promote dialogue among regional powers, including China, Japan, and the United States.

However, ASEAN faces challenges in maintaining its relevance and effectiveness. The consensus-based decision-making process can lead to slow responses to crises, as all members must agree before action can be taken. Additionally, ASEAN's commitment to non-interference has been criticized for limiting its ability to address human rights abuses and other internal issues within member states. Despite these challenges, ASEAN remains a key player in Southeast Asian affairs, providing a platform for regional cooperation and dialogue.

The African Union (AU), established in 2002 as the successor to the Organization of African Unity (OAU), aims to promote unity, peace, and development across the African continent. The AU's goals include promoting economic integration, defending the sovereignty and independence of its member states, and advancing democracy and human rights.

One of the AU's key initiatives is the African Continental Free Trade Area (AfCFTA), which seeks to create a single market for goods and services across Africa. Launched in 2021, the AfCFTA is expected to boost intra-African trade, promote industrialization, and foster economic growth. The AU also plays a critical role in conflict resolution and peacekeeping on the continent. Through its Peace and Security Council (PSC), the AU has authorized and conducted numerous peacekeeping missions, including in Darfur, Somalia, and the Central African Republic.

The AU's institutional structure includes the Assembly of the African Union, composed of heads of state and government, and the African Union Commission (AUC), which functions as the executive branch. The AU also has a Pan-African Parliament and various specialized agencies focused on issues such as health, education, and infrastructure. These institutions work together to implement the AU's vision of an integrated, prosperous, and peaceful Africa.

However, the AU faces significant challenges, including limited financial resources, weak enforcement mechanisms, and the diversity of its 55 member states. **Political instability, poverty, and human rights abuses remain pressing issues on the continent, and the AU has struggled to address these challenges effectively.** Nonetheless, the AU is an essential platform for promoting African unity and addressing continental issues, from conflict resolution to economic development.

CHAPTER 4: DIPLOMACY AND NEGOTIATION

History and Evolution of Diplomacy

Diplomacy has been a cornerstone of international relations for centuries, evolving alongside the development of states and the international system. **The origins of diplomacy can be traced back to ancient civilizations**, where rulers and states recognized the need for communication and negotiation to manage relations with their neighbors. Early forms of diplomacy were often ad hoc, conducted by envoys or messengers sent on specific missions to negotiate treaties, deliver messages, or resolve conflicts.

In ancient Mesopotamia and Egypt, diplomacy was used to manage relations between city-states and kingdoms. These early diplomatic efforts often focused on trade agreements, military alliances, and marriage treaties to secure peace and cooperation. The Amarna letters, a collection of diplomatic correspondence from the 14th century BCE between Egypt and other Near Eastern powers, provide a glimpse into how diplomacy was practiced in this period. These letters reveal the use of formalized language, negotiations over dowries and tribute, and the exchange of gifts to maintain friendly relations.

The classical civilizations of Greece and Rome further developed the practice of diplomacy. In ancient Greece, diplomacy was conducted by city-states (poleis) through the use of proxenoi, who acted as representatives or consuls in other cities. These diplomats were often citizens of the host city who represented the interests of their home city-state. Greek diplomacy focused on forming alliances, managing conflicts, and negotiating peace treaties, particularly during the Peloponnesian War. The Romans expanded the scope of diplomacy as they built their empire, establishing a more formalized system of envoys and ambassadors to manage relations with distant territories and foreign powers.

The fall of the Roman Empire and the rise of the Byzantine Empire saw diplomacy take on new importance. **The Byzantine Empire was known for its sophisticated and highly developed diplomatic practices**, which were crucial to its survival in a hostile environment. The Byzantines relied on a network of diplomats, spies, and informants to gather intelligence, negotiate treaties, and manage relations with neighboring states, including the Persians, Arabs, and various European powers. The Byzantine approach to diplomacy was pragmatic, often using bribes, marriages, and other forms of soft power to achieve its objectives without resorting to war.

During the Middle Ages, diplomacy in Europe was dominated by the Catholic Church and the feudal system. The Pope and other church leaders had key roles in mediating disputes between Christian rulers, while the feudal system required lords and vassals to negotiate complex networks of alliances and loyalties. Diplomatic practices during this period were relatively informal, with envoys and messengers playing a central role in communication between rulers.

The Renaissance marked a significant turning point in the history of diplomacy. **The rise of powerful city-states in Italy, such as Venice, Florence, and Milan, led to the development of modern diplomatic practices.** These city-states, engaged in intense competition for power and influence, began to establish permanent embassies in foreign capitals, staffed by resident ambassadors. The establishment of resident embassies allowed for continuous diplomatic presence and communication, which was a major innovation at the time. Ambassadors were expected to gather intelligence, negotiate on behalf of their state, and represent their ruler's interests abroad.

The Treaty of Westphalia in 1648, which ended the Thirty Years' War, is often cited as a key moment in the evolution of diplomacy. The treaty established the principles of state sovereignty and non-interference in the internal affairs of other states, which became foundational to modern international relations. The Westphalian system formalized the concept of diplomatic immunity, ensuring that ambassadors could carry out their duties without fear of arrest or harassment by the host country.

The 18th and 19th centuries saw further professionalization of diplomacy, with the establishment of foreign ministries and the standardization of diplomatic ranks and procedures. The Congress of Vienna (1814-1815), which sought to restore order to Europe after the Napoleonic Wars, is an example of multilateral diplomacy, where representatives from multiple states gathered to negotiate a comprehensive peace settlement. This period also saw the development of international law and the codification of diplomatic practices, such as the Vienna Convention on Diplomatic Relations in 1961, which formalized the rights and responsibilities of diplomats.

In the 20th century, diplomacy expanded beyond the traditional state-to-state model to include international organizations and non-state actors. The creation of the League of Nations after World War I and the United Nations after World War II reflected the growing importance of multilateral diplomacy in addressing global challenges. Today, diplomacy involves a wide range of issues, from trade and environmental agreements to human rights and security, reflecting the complexity of the modern international system.

Diplomacy has evolved from a practice focused on personal relationships between rulers to a highly structured and professionalized system of communication between states and other international actors. **Throughout its history, diplomacy has remained a vital tool for managing conflict, building alliances, and promoting cooperation in an increasingly interconnected world.**

Types of Diplomacy (Bilateral, Multilateral, Track II)

Diplomacy, the practice of managing international relations through dialogue and negotiation, takes various forms depending on the nature of the interactions and the number of parties involved. The most common types of diplomacy are bilateral, multilateral, and Track II diplomacy, each serving distinct purposes and functions within the international system.

Bilateral diplomacy involves direct communication and negotiation between two states. This form of diplomacy is the most traditional and remains the foundation of international relations. **Bilateral diplomacy allows states to address issues of mutual concern directly, tailor agreements to specific needs, and build strong bilateral relationships.** It is often conducted through embassies, where ambassadors and their staff engage with the host country's government to negotiate treaties, discuss trade agreements, resolve disputes, and promote their nation's interests.

Bilateral diplomacy is particularly effective for managing sensitive or complex issues that require a focused and nuanced approach. **For example, the negotiations between the United States and the Soviet Union during the Cold War, particularly on arms control, were conducted largely through bilateral channels.** The Strategic Arms Limitation Talks (SALT) and the subsequent treaties were the results of intense bilateral diplomacy, where both sides negotiated directly to manage their nuclear arsenals and reduce the risk of conflict.

Bilateral diplomacy also allows for the development of long-term relationships between states. These relationships can lead to increased trust and cooperation, making it easier to address future issues. **For instance, the close bilateral ties between the United States and the United Kingdom, often referred to as the "special relationship," have facilitated extensive cooperation in areas such as defense, intelligence, and trade.** However, bilateral diplomacy can also lead to imbalances of power, where a stronger state may exert undue influence over a weaker partner, sometimes leading to unequal agreements.

Multilateral diplomacy involves multiple states engaging in dialogue and negotiation, usually within the framework of international organizations or conferences. This type of diplomacy is essential for addressing global issues that require the cooperation of many countries, such as climate change, trade, and international security. **Multilateral diplomacy is characterized by its inclusiveness and the need to achieve consensus among diverse actors, making it both challenging and vital in the globalized world.**

The United Nations (UN) is the most prominent platform for multilateral diplomacy. The UN General Assembly, where all member states are represented, provides a forum for multilateral discussions on a wide range of global issues. **Multilateral diplomacy within the UN often involves complex negotiations, where states must balance their national interests with the need to reach agreements that are acceptable to a broad group of countries.** The Paris Agreement on climate change, negotiated under the UN Framework Convention on Climate Change (UNFCCC), is a prime example of successful multilateral diplomacy, where nearly every country in the world committed to reducing greenhouse gas emissions.

Multilateral diplomacy is also conducted within other international organizations, such as the World Trade Organization (WTO), the European Union (EU), and regional bodies like the African Union (AU) and the Association of Southeast Asian Nations (ASEAN). **These organizations provide frameworks for states to negotiate trade agreements, coordinate policies, and address regional conflicts.** While multilateral diplomacy can be slow and cumbersome, given the need for consensus among many participants, it is crucial for managing issues that transcend national borders.

Track II diplomacy refers to informal, non-governmental dialogue between states or other international actors. This form of diplomacy is conducted by private individuals, academics, NGOs, and other non-state actors who engage in discussions to help resolve conflicts or build relationships between adversaries. **Track II diplomacy is particularly useful in situations where official, government-led negotiations have stalled or where there is a need to explore new ideas and approaches in a less formal setting.**

Track II diplomacy allows participants to discuss sensitive issues without the pressure of official positions or the fear of political repercussions. **This can lead to more open and creative discussions, where parties can explore solutions that might not be feasible in formal negotiations.** For example, during the Israeli-Palestinian conflict, Track II initiatives have provided valuable backchannel communication that has helped to keep dialogue open even when official talks have broken down.

Track II diplomacy is not limited to conflict resolution. It can also play a role in fostering mutual understanding and cooperation on broader issues, such as human rights, environmental protection, and cultural exchange. **Organizations like the Council for Security Cooperation in the Asia Pacific (CSCAP) engage in Track II diplomacy to promote dialogue on security issues in the Asia-Pacific region, involving academics, policymakers, and experts from various countries.**

While Track II diplomacy does not have the same formal authority as government-led diplomacy, it can influence official negotiations by shaping the agenda, building trust, and generating new ideas. **In some cases, Track II initiatives have paved the way for formal agreements, serving as a precursor to official Track I**

negotiations. However, the informal nature of Track II diplomacy also means that it may not always lead to concrete outcomes, as it lacks the binding power of official agreements.

The Art of Negotiation in IR

Negotiation is at the heart of international relations, serving as the primary means by which states and other actors resolve disputes, forge agreements, and manage their interactions. **The art of negotiation in international relations involves a complex assortment of strategy, communication, and diplomacy, where the goal is to achieve outcomes that align with a state's interests while maintaining relationships and stability.**

Successful negotiation begins with preparation. Before entering into negotiations, states must clearly define their objectives, understand their priorities, and identify potential areas of compromise. This involves a thorough analysis of the issue at hand, the interests of the other parties involved, and the broader geopolitical context. **Negotiators must also consider their own strengths and weaknesses, as well as those of their counterparts.** This preparation is key, as it allows negotiators to enter discussions with a clear understanding of what they want to achieve and how they might get there. **National leaders seek to take advantage of the weaknesses of other countries and expect leaders from other countries to do the same toward them. This type of interaction is generally considered to be unacceptable at the personal level but is common in international relations.**

One of the key strategies in negotiation is the establishment of a strong position. This involves making a compelling case for one's interests and demonstrating the value of one's proposals. However, a strong position must be balanced with flexibility. Negotiators need to be prepared to make concessions and adjust their demands in response to the dynamics of the negotiation process. This requires a deep understanding of both the issues at stake and the perspectives of the other parties. A rigid, uncompromising stance can lead to deadlock, while excessive concessions can undermine a state's interests and credibility.

Communication is another critical component of successful negotiation. This goes beyond simply stating positions; it involves active listening, asking questions, and responding thoughtfully to the concerns and arguments of the other parties. Effective communication helps to build trust, clarify misunderstandings, and create a more collaborative atmosphere. **It also involves non-verbal cues, such as body language and tone of voice, which can convey confidence, openness, or even subtle pressure.** Skilled negotiators use communication to shape the narrative of the negotiation, framing issues in ways that make their proposals more appealing or highlighting the costs of inaction or failure to agree.

Timing is also crucial in negotiation. Knowing when to push forward, when to hold back, and when to make a decisive move can greatly influence the outcome. Negotiators must be attuned to the pace of the discussions, recognizing when a window of opportunity opens or when it is better to delay a decision until more favorable conditions arise. **This sense of timing is often developed through experience and a keen understanding of the negotiation's context, including the domestic pressures facing each party and the broader international environment.**

Power dynamics have a significant role in negotiations. States with greater economic, military, or diplomatic power often have an advantage, as they can exert pressure or offer incentives that less powerful states cannot match. However, power is not always about size or strength. Smaller states or those with fewer resources can leverage other forms of power, such as alliances, moral authority, or expertise on specific issues. **For example, small island states have successfully used their moral authority and expertise on climate change to influence international negotiations, despite their limited traditional power.**

One of the most challenging aspects of negotiation is managing conflict and disagreement. Disputes are inevitable in any negotiation, particularly when the stakes are high or the issues are deeply contentious. Skilled negotiators must navigate these conflicts without allowing them to derail the process. This often involves finding common ground, reframing issues to make them more palatable, or seeking compromises that satisfy the core interests of all parties. In some cases, it may also involve using third-party mediators to help bridge gaps and facilitate communication.

The use of leverage is another important tactic in negotiation. Leverage refers to the tools or advantages a negotiator can use to influence the outcome. This could include economic incentives, security guarantees, or the threat of sanctions or other consequences. **Leverage is most effective when it is applied strategically, with a clear understanding of what will motivate the other party to agree.** However, it must be used carefully, as excessive pressure can lead to resistance, backlash, or even the breakdown of negotiations.

Negotiations often conclude with the drafting of an agreement. This agreement must be carefully worded to ensure that it accurately reflects the terms agreed upon and that it is acceptable to all parties involved. The language of the agreement is critical, as ambiguities or poorly defined terms can lead to misunderstandings or disputes in the future. **Once an agreement is reached, the next challenge is ensuring its implementation and compliance.** This may require ongoing monitoring, enforcement mechanisms, and sometimes further negotiations to address unforeseen issues or to adapt the agreement to changing circumstances.

In international relations, the art of negotiation is not just about winning or getting the best deal. It is about managing relationships, maintaining stability, and finding solutions that are sustainable and mutually acceptable. Negotiators must balance the pursuit of their state's interests with the need to preserve trust and cooperation, which are essential for future interactions. **The ability to negotiate effectively is a key skill for diplomats and policymakers, as it enables them to navigate the complexities of international politics and achieve their objectives in a challenging and often unpredictable environment.**

The Role of Diplomats and Embassies

Diplomats and embassies are the backbone of international relations, serving as the primary means through which states communicate, negotiate, and maintain relationships with one another. **The role of diplomats and embassies is multifaceted, encompassing everything from representing their country abroad to protecting the interests of their citizens and promoting trade, culture, and cooperation.**

Diplomats are the official representatives of their state in a foreign country or within an international organization. Their primary role is to maintain and manage diplomatic relations between their home country and the host nation. This involves a wide range of activities, including negotiating treaties, representing their country's position on various issues, and working to resolve conflicts or disputes. Diplomats must navigate complex political landscapes, balancing the interests of their own government with the realities of the host country's political, economic, and social environment.

One of the key responsibilities of diplomats is to gather information and provide analysis on developments in the host country. This intelligence-gathering function is crucial for informing their home government's foreign policy decisions. Diplomats monitor political events, economic trends, and social movements, providing regular reports that help their government understand the host country's internal dynamics and predict potential challenges or opportunities. This information is often used to shape diplomatic strategies and to prepare for negotiations or other interactions with the host country.

Diplomats also play a critical role in protecting the interests of their country and its citizens abroad. This includes assisting nationals who are traveling or living in the host country, such as providing consular services, helping in legal matters, or offering assistance during emergencies. In times of crisis, such as natural disasters or political unrest, diplomats may coordinate evacuation efforts or provide support to citizens in distress. The protection of citizens is a fundamental aspect of diplomatic work, reflecting the responsibility of the state to safeguard its nationals wherever they may be.

Embassies are the physical embodiments of diplomacy. They serve as the headquarters for a country's diplomatic mission in a foreign nation and are typically located in the host country's capital. Embassies are staffed by diplomats, consular officers, and other personnel who carry out the various functions of the diplomatic mission. **The ambassador, who leads the embassy, is the highest-ranking diplomat and serves as the personal representative of the head of state of the sending country.**

Embassies perform a wide range of functions beyond traditional diplomacy. They are centers for cultural exchange, economic promotion, and public diplomacy. Embassies often host cultural events, sponsor educational programs, and promote the sending country's culture and values. These activities help build goodwill and foster mutual understanding between the people of the host country and the sending country. Economic diplomacy is another key function, where embassies work to promote trade and investment, support businesses, and negotiate economic agreements that benefit their home country.

In addition to their diplomatic and consular functions, embassies also serve as hubs for international cooperation. They facilitate collaboration on global issues such as climate change, public health, and security. Embassies often work closely with international organizations, NGOs, and other stakeholders to address these challenges, reflecting the interconnected nature of modern diplomacy.

Diplomats must also navigate the complexities of protocol and etiquette. Diplomatic protocol involves the rules and customs that govern interactions between states and their representatives. This includes everything from the order of precedence at official events to the appropriate forms of address and the conduct of negotiations. **Adhering to protocol is essential for maintaining respect and good relations between states, as breaches of protocol can lead to misunderstandings or even diplomatic incidents.**

The role of diplomats and embassies has evolved with the changing nature of international relations. In the past, diplomacy was often conducted behind closed doors, with a focus on secrecy and the negotiation of treaties. Today, diplomacy is more transparent and multifaceted, involving a broader range of actors and issues. Diplomats now engage with civil society, businesses, and the public, reflecting the growing importance of soft power and public diplomacy. Embassies are increasingly involved in promoting sustainable development, human rights, and global cooperation, aligning their activities with the broader goals of international peace and stability.

Despite the many changes in the practice of diplomacy, the core functions of diplomats and embassies remain essential. They are the face of their country abroad, working to protect and promote their nation's interests while building and maintaining the relationships that are crucial for international peace and cooperation.

CHAPTER 5: SECURITY STUDIES IN INTERNATIONAL RELATIONS

Traditional vs. Non-Traditional Security

Traditional security in international relations focuses on the protection of states from external threats, primarily through military means. This concept of security is rooted in the idea that the primary responsibility of a state is to defend its sovereignty, territorial integrity, and political independence. **In traditional security, the main concern is the threat of war and armed conflict between states.** This has been the dominant understanding of security for much of history, especially during periods like the Cold War when the possibility of large-scale military conflict between superpowers was a constant concern.

The traditional security paradigm is state-centric. It assumes that states are the primary actors in international relations and that the most significant threats to security come from other states. Military power, alliances, and deterrence strategies are central to this approach. The concept of balance of power, where states seek to maintain stability by preventing any one state from becoming too dominant, is a key component of traditional security thinking. Nuclear deterrence during the Cold War is a classic example of traditional security in action, where the threat of mutually assured destruction (MAD) was used to prevent a direct conflict between the United States and the Soviet Union.

In contrast, **non-traditional security** expands the definition of security to include a broader range of threats that do not necessarily involve military force or state actors. Non-traditional security issues include challenges such as terrorism, environmental degradation, pandemics, human trafficking, and cyber threats. **These issues often cross national borders, making them transnational in nature and requiring international cooperation to address.** Unlike traditional security threats, which are usually external and state-centric, non-traditional security threats can be internal, involve non-state actors, and impact both state and individual levels.

Terrorism is a prime example of a non-traditional security threat. It is not confined by national borders and often involves non-state actors, such as terrorist organizations or networks. The attacks of September 11, 2001, highlighted the global nature of terrorism and led to a shift in security strategies worldwide. Governments began to focus more on intelligence gathering, international cooperation, and counterterrorism measures, recognizing that traditional military responses alone were insufficient to address the threat of terrorism.

Environmental security is another critical area of non-traditional security. Climate change, deforestation, and pollution pose significant risks to global stability.

These environmental issues can lead to resource scarcity, forced migration, and conflict over resources such as water and arable land. **The concept of environmental security recognizes that the degradation of natural resources and ecosystems can undermine national and global security, leading to social unrest, economic instability, and even conflict.** For instance, the impact of climate change on agriculture and water resources in regions like the Sahel has been linked to increased tensions and conflicts.

Health security has also gained prominence, particularly in light of global pandemics such as COVID-19. Health security focuses on protecting populations from infectious diseases, ensuring access to healthcare, and maintaining public health systems. The rapid spread of COVID-19 underscored the importance of international cooperation in managing health crises, as no country can effectively combat a global pandemic in isolation. **The pandemic also highlighted the interconnectedness of global health with economic and social stability, showing how health issues can quickly become security issues when they disrupt societies and economies.**

Cybersecurity is a rapidly emerging non-traditional security concern. The increasing reliance on digital infrastructure makes states, businesses, and individuals vulnerable to cyberattacks, which can disrupt critical systems, steal sensitive information, and even influence political processes. Cybersecurity challenges traditional notions of security because the threats often come from non-state actors, such as hackers or criminal organizations, and the attacks can be difficult to attribute or respond to using traditional military means.

Non-traditional security requires a multi-dimensional approach that goes beyond military power. It involves economic policies, environmental management, public health strategies, and international cooperation. This broader understanding of security recognizes that threats to stability and well-being can come from a wide range of sources, many of which are interconnected and cannot be addressed by any single country alone.

While traditional and non-traditional security are distinct, they are not mutually exclusive. Both are essential for a comprehensive understanding of global security. The traditional focus on military threats and state sovereignty remains relevant, particularly in areas of ongoing conflict or where state actors pose direct threats to each other. However, the rise of non-traditional security issues reflects the changing nature of global challenges in the 21st century, where threats are more diffuse, transnational, and often involve non-state actors.

The Concept of National Security

National security is a fundamental concept in international relations, referring to the protection and preservation of a nation's sovereignty, territorial integrity, and political independence from external and internal threats. Traditionally, national security has been understood in terms of military defense against foreign aggression. However, the concept has evolved to encompass a broader range of issues, reflecting the complex and interconnected nature of contemporary global challenges.

At its core, national security involves safeguarding a state's vital interests. These interests include the protection of its citizens, the preservation of its political and economic systems, and the maintenance of its territorial boundaries. Historically, the primary focus of national security was on military power and the ability to defend against external threats, such as invasions or attacks by other states. During the Cold War, for example, national security was largely defined by the need to deter or respond to potential military conflicts between superpowers, particularly the United States and the Soviet Union.

The traditional military-centric view of national security has been complemented by the recognition of other critical dimensions. Economic security, for instance, is now considered an integral part of national security. A nation's economic stability and prosperity are essential for its overall security, as economic weakness can lead to political instability, social unrest, and vulnerability to external pressures. Economic security also involves protecting critical infrastructure, such as energy supplies, transportation networks, and financial systems, from disruption or sabotage.

In addition to military and economic security, political security is another crucial aspect of national security. This involves the protection of a nation's political institutions, governance structures, and democratic processes from internal and external threats. Political security is essential for maintaining the legitimacy and stability of the state, as well as for ensuring the effective functioning of its government. Threats to political security can come from various sources, including terrorism, political extremism, foreign interference, and internal dissent.

The concept of national security has also expanded to include societal and environmental dimensions. Societal security refers to the protection of a nation's cultural identity, social cohesion, and the well-being of its citizens. This includes addressing issues such as social inequality, ethnic tensions, and the protection of minority rights. Environmental security, on the other hand, focuses on the protection of natural resources and ecosystems, recognizing that environmental degradation and climate change can pose significant threats to national security. For example, rising sea levels, extreme weather events, and resource scarcity can lead to displacement, conflict, and instability.

Cybersecurity has emerged as a critical component of national security in the digital age. As nations increasingly rely on digital infrastructure for communication, commerce, and governance, the protection of this infrastructure from cyberattacks has become a top priority. Cyber threats can come from state and non-state actors, including hackers, criminal organizations, and foreign governments. These threats can disrupt essential services, steal sensitive information, and even undermine democratic processes, such as elections.

The concept of national security is also shaped by the evolving nature of global threats and the interconnectedness of the international system. Globalization, technological advances, and the rise of non-state actors have blurred the lines between domestic and international security, making it more challenging to define and address national security threats. For example, the spread of global terrorism, pandemics, and transnational organized crime requires coordinated efforts at the national, regional, and international levels.

In response to these challenges, national security strategies have become more comprehensive and integrated. Governments now recognize the need to adopt a multidimensional approach to national security, one that addresses both traditional and non-traditional threats. This includes strengthening military capabilities, enhancing economic resilience, protecting critical infrastructure, and promoting social cohesion. It also involves fostering international cooperation, as many national security threats are transnational and require collective action.

Overall, national security is a dynamic and evolving concept that encompasses a wide range of issues beyond just military defense. It reflects the need to protect a nation's vital interests in a complex and interconnected world, where threats can come from multiple sources and take many forms. Understanding and addressing these diverse aspects of national security is essential for maintaining the stability, prosperity, and sovereignty of states in the 21st century.

Global Terrorism and Counterterrorism Strategies

Global terrorism is one of the most pressing security challenges of the 21st century, affecting nations across the world. Terrorism involves the use of violence or the threat of violence to achieve political, ideological, or religious objectives. **What distinguishes terrorism from other forms of violence is its deliberate targeting of civilians and its aim to instill fear and achieve maximum psychological impact.** The global nature of terrorism, with networks that operate across borders, has necessitated the development of comprehensive counterterrorism strategies that involve a range of military, political, legal, and societal measures.

The roots of global terrorism are complex and multifaceted, often involving a mix of political, economic, social, and religious factors. Many terrorist groups, such as Al-Qaeda and ISIS, have emerged in regions marked by political instability, economic deprivation, and social marginalization. These groups exploit grievances, whether real or perceived, to recruit members, gain support, and justify their actions. **Religious extremism has also had a key role in the rise of global terrorism, particularly in the case of jihadist groups that claim to fight in the name of Islam.** However, it is essential to recognize that terrorism is not confined to any one religion or ideology; it can be found across the political and ideological spectrum, including right-wing extremism, separatism, and left-wing radicalism.

Counterterrorism strategies must therefore be multifaceted, addressing the root causes of terrorism as well as its manifestations. One of the primary components of counterterrorism is the use of military force. Military operations, such as drone strikes, special forces missions, and air campaigns, are often used to target terrorist leaders, destroy training camps, and disrupt logistical networks. **However, military action alone is not sufficient to defeat terrorism.** It can sometimes lead to unintended consequences, such as civilian casualties, which can fuel further radicalization and recruitment. Therefore, military efforts must be carefully calibrated and complemented by other measures.

Intelligence gathering is a critical element of counterterrorism. Effective counterterrorism relies on timely and accurate intelligence to identify threats, track terrorist activities, and prevent attacks. This involves the use of advanced surveillance technologies, human intelligence (HUMINT), and cooperation between domestic and international intelligence agencies. The sharing of intelligence between countries is important in the fight against global terrorism, as terrorist networks often operate across borders and maintain connections in multiple countries. The success of counterterrorism operations, such as the killing of Osama bin Laden in 2011, often hinges on the quality and coordination of intelligence efforts.

Legal and law enforcement measures are also vital in counterterrorism. Governments must develop and enforce laws that criminalize terrorist activities, financing, and recruitment. This includes freezing the assets of individuals and organizations linked to terrorism, prosecuting those involved in terrorist plots, and preventing the spread of extremist ideologies through the internet and other media. Law enforcement agencies are important in monitoring and disrupting terrorist activities within their borders, often working in tandem with intelligence services to prevent attacks before they occur.

Addressing the ideological and social dimensions of terrorism is another essential component of counterterrorism strategies. Efforts to counter violent extremism (CVE) focus on preventing the radicalization of individuals and communities, particularly those most vulnerable to terrorist recruitment. This involves promoting counter-narratives that challenge the propaganda of terrorist groups, supporting moderate voices within communities, and addressing the socio-economic conditions that contribute to radicalization. Programs aimed at education, community engagement, and social inclusion are critical in this regard, as they help to build resilience against extremist ideologies.

International cooperation is crucial in the fight against global terrorism. Terrorism is a transnational threat that requires coordinated efforts at the global, regional, and national levels. International organizations, such as the United Nations, the European Union, and INTERPOL, play important roles in facilitating cooperation, sharing best practices, and coordinating counterterrorism initiatives. For example, the UN Global Counter-Terrorism Strategy provides a comprehensive framework for international action, emphasizing the need for a balanced approach that includes measures to prevent and combat terrorism while respecting human rights and the rule of law.

Despite these efforts, counterterrorism strategies face significant challenges. The decentralized nature of many terrorist networks makes them difficult to dismantle, and the rise of "lone wolf" attackers—individuals who act independently but are inspired by terrorist ideologies—complicates detection and prevention efforts. The use of the internet and social media by terrorist groups for recruitment, propaganda, and coordination also presents new challenges for counterterrorism efforts, requiring innovative approaches to monitor and counter online radicalization.

Nuclear Proliferation and Arms Control

Nuclear proliferation refers to the spread of nuclear weapons and technology to states that do not already possess them. **The potential for the widespread use of nuclear weapons poses one of the most significant threats to global security.** Since the first use of nuclear weapons in World War II, the international community has sought to control the spread of these weapons and reduce the risk of nuclear conflict.

The Cold War era was marked by intense nuclear rivalry between the United States and the Soviet Union. Both superpowers amassed large arsenals of nuclear weapons, leading to a tense standoff known as mutually assured destruction (MAD). The logic of MAD suggested that the possession of large, survivable nuclear arsenals by both sides would deter either from launching a first strike, as it would lead to their own annihilation. However, this arms race also led to the proliferation of nuclear weapons, as other countries sought to develop their own arsenals for security reasons.

To prevent further proliferation, the international community established several key arms control agreements. The most significant of these is the Treaty on the Non-Proliferation of Nuclear Weapons (NPT), which was opened for signature in 1968 and came into force in 1970. The NPT has three main pillars:

non-proliferation, disarmament, and the peaceful use of nuclear energy. **Under the NPT, nuclear-armed states agree not to transfer nuclear weapons or technology to non-nuclear states, while non-nuclear states agree not to pursue nuclear weapons.** In return, all states have the right to access nuclear technology for peaceful purposes, such as energy production.

While the NPT has been successful in limiting the number of nuclear-armed states, it has not completely halted proliferation. Countries like India, Pakistan, and North Korea have developed nuclear weapons outside the framework of the NPT, while others, such as Iran, have been suspected of pursuing nuclear weapons under the guise of peaceful nuclear programs. The challenge of enforcing compliance with the NPT and verifying that states are not secretly developing nuclear weapons remains a significant issue. International bodies like the International Atomic Energy Agency (IAEA) are important in monitoring compliance, but their effectiveness depends on the cooperation of member states.

In addition to the NPT, other arms control agreements have sought to limit the number and types of nuclear weapons. The Strategic Arms Reduction Treaty (START) series, initially signed between the United States and the Soviet Union (and later Russia), aimed to reduce the number of deployed strategic nuclear warheads. These treaties have led to significant reductions in nuclear arsenals, although challenges remain in ensuring compliance and adapting to new technological developments, such as missile defense systems and hypersonic weapons.

Nuclear disarmament remains a long-term goal of the international community, though progress has been slow and uneven. Some countries, particularly those in the Non-Aligned Movement, advocate for the complete elimination of nuclear weapons. In contrast, nuclear-armed states often argue that their arsenals are necessary for deterrence and national security. The Treaty on the Prohibition of Nuclear Weapons (TPNW), adopted in 2017, represents a more recent effort to achieve nuclear disarmament by explicitly banning the use, development, and possession of nuclear weapons. **However, major nuclear powers have not joined the TPNW, limiting its impact.**

The threat of nuclear proliferation is compounded by the risk of nuclear weapons falling into the hands of non-state actors, such as terrorist groups. Preventing nuclear terrorism requires robust security measures to protect nuclear materials and technology and international cooperation to track and intercept illicit nuclear trade.

While significant progress has been made in limiting the spread of nuclear weapons and reducing arsenals, ongoing challenges and the emergence of new threats highlight the need for continued vigilance and cooperation in this area.

Cybersecurity as a New Dimension of Security

Cybersecurity has emerged as a critical dimension of security in the digital age, as states, businesses, and individuals increasingly rely on digital networks and infrastructure. **The growing dependence on information technology has created new vulnerabilities, making cybersecurity an essential aspect of national and international security.** Cyber threats range from hacking and data breaches to cyber espionage and the disruption of critical infrastructure, all of which can have significant political, economic, and social consequences.

Cybersecurity differs from traditional security in that the threats are often invisible and can originate from non-state actors. Unlike conventional military threats, which typically involve identifiable adversaries and physical conflict, cyber threats can be launched by individuals, criminal organizations, or state-sponsored actors operating anonymously from anywhere in the world. **This anonymity complicates the attribution of cyberattacks, making it difficult to respond or hold perpetrators accountable.** For instance, cyberattacks like the 2017 WannaCry ransomware attack and the 2020 SolarWinds hack were attributed to state-sponsored actors, but conclusive attribution and response remained complex.

Critical infrastructure, such as power grids, financial systems, and communication networks, are particularly vulnerable to cyberattacks. Disruptions to these systems can have cascading effects, crippling economies, endangering public safety, and undermining national security. In 2015, a cyberattack on Ukraine's power grid left over 200,000 people without electricity, highlighting the real-world impact of cyber threats. As such, protecting critical infrastructure from cyber threats has become a top priority for governments worldwide.

Cyber espionage is another significant concern in cybersecurity. States and non-state actors use cyber tools to steal sensitive information, including intellectual property, trade secrets, and government communications. **Cyber espionage can undermine national security, weaken economies, and erode trust between nations.** The theft of intellectual property, particularly by state-sponsored actors, has been a point of contention in international relations, leading to accusations, sanctions, and calls for stronger cybersecurity measures.

The rise of cyber warfare adds another layer of complexity to international security. Cyber warfare involves the use of cyberattacks to achieve strategic objectives, such as disabling military systems, disrupting command and control networks, or manipulating information. **As cyber capabilities become more sophisticated, the potential for cyber warfare to escalate into broader conflicts increases.** For example, the Stuxnet worm, discovered in 2010, was a highly sophisticated cyber weapon that targeted Iran's nuclear program, causing significant damage without a single shot being fired. This incident demonstrated how cyber tools could be used to achieve strategic goals with minimal physical engagement.

International cooperation is crucial for addressing cybersecurity threats, as these threats often transcend national borders. The global nature of cyberspace means that no single country can effectively secure its digital infrastructure alone. International organizations, such as the United Nations and the European Union, have begun to develop frameworks for cybersecurity cooperation, but significant challenges remain. Differences in national cybersecurity policies, legal frameworks, and levels of technological development make it difficult to establish common standards and practices. Moreover, the lack of a clear consensus on norms and rules for state behavior in cyberspace further complicates efforts to prevent and respond to cyber threats.

In addition to state-led efforts, the private sector is important in cybersecurity. Many critical infrastructures are owned and operated by private companies, making their cybersecurity practices essential for national security. Public-private partnerships are therefore vital for enhancing cybersecurity, as governments and businesses must work together to protect digital networks and respond to cyber incidents. Additionally, the rapid pace of technological innovation means that cybersecurity strategies must constantly evolve to address new threats and vulnerabilities.

Education and awareness are also key components of effective cybersecurity. Individuals and organizations must be educated about the risks of cyber threats and the best practices for protecting their information. **Simple measures, such as using strong passwords, keeping software up to date, and being vigilant against phishing attacks, can significantly reduce the risk of cyber incidents.** Governments and businesses are increasingly investing in cybersecurity training and awareness programs to build a more resilient digital environment.

CHAPTER 6: CONFLICT AND COOPERATION IN INTERNATIONAL RELATIONS

Causes of International Conflicts

International conflicts arise from a variety of causes, reflecting the complex and often competing interests of states and other international actors. Understanding these causes is crucial for analyzing why conflicts occur and how they might be prevented or resolved.

Power and security are central drivers of international conflicts. States exist in an anarchic international system where no central authority enforces rules or guarantees security. This environment leads to a security dilemma, where the actions taken by one state to enhance its security, such as increasing military capabilities, can be perceived as a threat by other states. This perception can lead to an arms race or even preemptive strikes, as states seek to protect themselves from potential aggression. The Cold War is a classic example, where the United States and the Soviet Union engaged in an arms race fueled by mutual fear and suspicion, ultimately leading to numerous proxy wars and global tensions.

Territorial disputes are another common cause of international conflict. States may contest borders or claim the same piece of land, often due to its strategic importance, natural resources, or historical significance. These disputes can lead to protracted conflicts, especially when both sides view the territory as vital to their national identity or survival. The conflict between India and Pakistan over the Kashmir region is a long-standing example, where both countries claim sovereignty over the area, leading to several wars and ongoing military tensions.

Economic interests often drive conflicts as well. Access to resources such as oil, water, and minerals can become a significant source of tension between states, especially in regions where resources are scarce. Economic conflicts can also arise from trade disputes, competition for markets, and differences over economic policies. For instance, the conflict in the South China Sea involves several countries claiming overlapping maritime territories rich in natural resources, leading to heightened tensions and military confrontations.

Nationalism and ideology can fuel conflicts by exacerbating divisions between states or groups within states. Nationalistic fervor often leads to aggressive foreign policies, as leaders use national identity and pride to justify expansionist goals or to rally public support for conflict. Ideological conflicts, such as those seen during the Cold War, pit different political or economic systems against each other, with each side seeking to spread its ideology and suppress the other. The Korean War, for example, was driven by the ideological clash between communism and capitalism, with the Korean Peninsula becoming a battleground for these competing visions.

Ethnic and religious differences can also lead to international conflicts, particularly when groups seek autonomy or independence. These conflicts often cross borders, drawing in neighboring states that support one side or another, either due to shared ethnicity, religion, or strategic interests. The breakup of Yugoslavia in the 1990s resulted in several ethnically driven conflicts, as different groups sought to establish their own states, leading to international interventions and widespread violence.

Historical grievances and unresolved disputes often linger and can reignite conflicts. Past wars, colonialism, and injustices can leave deep scars, with memories of these events fueling future conflicts. States or groups may seek to right perceived wrongs, reclaim lost territories, or exact revenge for past humiliations. The Israeli-Palestinian conflict, deeply rooted in historical grievances, continues to be one of the most enduring and intractable conflicts in the world.

Internal political instability and regime change can spill over into international conflicts. Weak or failing states may become battlegrounds for external powers seeking to influence outcomes, support factions, or prevent the spread of instability. The Syrian Civil War, which began as an internal conflict, quickly drew in regional and global powers, turning the country into a proxy battlefield with significant international implications.

The role of alliances and external interventions can also exacerbate conflicts. When states form alliances, they often commit to defending each other, which can draw multiple countries into a conflict that might otherwise have remained localized. External interventions, whether in the form of military support, economic aid, or political pressure, can escalate conflicts by emboldening one side or making a negotiated settlement more difficult to achieve. The First World War is a historical example where a network of alliances led to a regional conflict in the Balkans expanding into a global war.

These causes of international conflicts are often interrelated, with multiple factors contributing to the outbreak of hostilities. Understanding these causes provides insight into the dynamics of international relations and the challenges of maintaining peace and stability in a complex and competitive world.

War and Peace Theories

War and peace theories in international relations seek to explain why conflicts occur and how lasting peace can be achieved. These theories offer different perspectives on the causes of war and the conditions necessary for peace, reflecting the complexity of global interactions.

Realism is one of the most influential theories explaining the causes of war. Realists view the international system as anarchic, meaning there is no central authority to enforce rules or protect states. In this environment, states must rely on their own power to ensure survival, leading to a constant struggle for security. Realists argue that this competition for power and security often results in war, as states seek to protect themselves or expand their influence. The balance of power is a central concept in realism, where states align themselves with others to prevent any single state from becoming too powerful. When this balance is disrupted, war may become more likely as states attempt to restore equilibrium.

Liberalism offers a more optimistic view, suggesting that war can be avoided through cooperation and the spread of democratic values. Liberals believe that democratic states are less likely to go to war with each other, a concept known as the Democratic Peace Theory. This theory posits that democracies are more transparent, accountable to their citizens, and inclined to resolve conflicts through negotiation rather than force. Liberalism also emphasizes the role of international institutions in promoting peace by providing frameworks for cooperation, dispute resolution, and collective security. The United Nations, for example, is important in preventing conflicts through peacekeeping missions and facilitating diplomatic negotiations.

Constructivism focuses on the role of ideas, identities, and norms in shaping state behavior and international relations. Constructivists argue that the causes of war and the prospects for peace are not solely determined by material factors, such as military power or economic resources, but also by the beliefs and perceptions of states and their leaders. For example, if states perceive each other as friends, they are more likely to cooperate and maintain peace. Conversely, if they view each other as enemies, conflict becomes more likely. Constructivists believe that changing the way states perceive each other can lead to a more peaceful world.

Marxism, on the other hand, views war as a result of economic inequalities and the capitalist system. Marxists argue that wars are often fought to protect or expand the economic interests of powerful states or corporations. **According to this perspective, imperialism and the competition for resources and markets drive conflicts, particularly between developed and developing nations.** Marxist theories suggest that global peace can only be achieved through the overthrow of capitalism and the establishment of a more equitable economic system.

The Just War Theory provides a moral framework for evaluating when it is justifiable to go to war and how wars should be conducted. This theory has its roots in classical and Christian philosophy, particularly in the works of Augustine and Thomas Aquinas. **Just War Theory outlines specific criteria that must be**

met for a war to be considered just, including just cause, legitimate authority, right intention, and proportionality. Additionally, it emphasizes the importance of distinguishing between combatants and non-combatants and avoiding unnecessary harm to civilians.

Theories of peacebuilding focus on the conditions necessary for achieving and sustaining peace after a conflict. These theories emphasize the importance of addressing the root causes of conflict, such as poverty, inequality, and social injustice, and promoting reconciliation, economic development, and the rule of law. Peacebuilding efforts often involve a combination of political, economic, and social strategies aimed at creating a stable and peaceful society.

In summary, war and peace theories offer different explanations for the causes of conflict and the pathways to peace. While realism emphasizes the inevitability of conflict in an anarchic world, liberalism, constructivism, and Marxism offer alternative perspectives that highlight the potential for cooperation, the influence of ideas, and the impact of economic factors on global stability. Understanding these theories is key for analyzing international relations and developing strategies to prevent war and promote lasting peace.

Conflict Resolution and Peacebuilding

Conflict resolution and peacebuilding are essential processes in international relations aimed at ending conflicts and establishing lasting peace. These processes involve a range of strategies, from diplomatic negotiations to post-conflict reconstruction, and require the cooperation of various stakeholders, including governments, international organizations, and civil society.

Conflict resolution is the process of addressing the underlying causes of a conflict and finding a mutually acceptable solution for all parties involved. This often involves negotiation, mediation, and diplomacy. Negotiation is a direct dialogue between the conflicting parties to reach an agreement. It requires compromise, trust-building, and a willingness to understand the other side's perspective. Successful negotiations often lead to peace agreements or treaties that outline the terms for ending the conflict and establishing peace.

Mediation is another key tool in conflict resolution, where a neutral third party helps facilitate negotiations between conflicting parties. Mediators work to de-escalate tensions, foster communication, and guide the parties toward a peaceful settlement. International organizations like the United Nations often play a mediating role in conflicts, offering their good offices and expertise to support peace processes. For instance, the UN has mediated conflicts in places like Cyprus, Sudan, and the Middle East, helping to negotiate ceasefires and peace agreements.

Peacebuilding goes beyond conflict resolution by focusing on creating the conditions necessary for a sustainable peace after the conflict has ended. This involves addressing the root causes of conflict, rebuilding institutions, and promoting reconciliation among former adversaries. Peacebuilding aims to prevent the recurrence of violence by strengthening governance, ensuring justice, and fostering economic development.

One of the critical aspects of peacebuilding is disarmament, demobilization, and reintegration (DDR) of former combatants. DDR programs help former fighters transition back into civilian life by providing them with education, vocational training, and other forms of support. Successful DDR programs can reduce the risk of ex-combatants returning to violence and contribute to the stability of post-conflict societies.

Reconciliation is another crucial component of peacebuilding. Reconciliation efforts seek to heal the wounds of conflict and rebuild trust between communities. **This can involve truth and reconciliation commissions, which allow victims and perpetrators to share their stories, acknowledge the past, and seek forgiveness.** South Africa's Truth and Reconciliation Commission is a notable example, where the process of truth-telling and forgiveness played a vital role in the country's transition from apartheid to democracy.

Economic development is also essential for peacebuilding. Post-conflict societies often face significant economic challenges, including poverty, unemployment, and damaged infrastructure. Economic reconstruction efforts focus on rebuilding infrastructure, creating jobs, and revitalizing the economy to provide a stable foundation for peace. International aid and development agencies are important in supporting these efforts by providing financial resources, technical assistance, and expertise.

Institutional reform is necessary to create a stable and just society after a conflict. This can involve reforming the security sector, establishing the rule of law, and ensuring that political institutions are inclusive and representative. Building strong institutions that can manage conflicts peacefully is important for preventing the recurrence of violence and ensuring long-term stability.

Peacebuilding is a long-term process that requires sustained commitment and resources. It often takes years, if not decades, to fully recover from a conflict and build a peaceful society. International support is vital for peacebuilding efforts, as many post-conflict countries lack the resources and capacity to rebuild on their own. The international community can provide financial assistance, technical expertise, and political support to help countries navigate the challenges of post-conflict reconstruction.

In sum, conflict resolution and peacebuilding are critical processes for ending conflicts and establishing lasting peace. They involve a combination of diplomatic efforts, reconciliation, economic development, and institutional reform, and require the cooperation of various stakeholders. While these processes are challenging and complex, they are essential for creating a stable and peaceful world.

Alliances and Collective Security

Alliances and collective security are key concepts in international relations that are important in maintaining peace and stability among states. **These concepts involve the cooperation of states to enhance their security and protect against common threats.** While alliances are often based on mutual interests and commitments, collective security represents a broader framework for maintaining international peace through cooperation among many states.

Alliances are formal agreements between two or more states to cooperate on security matters. These agreements often involve commitments to mutual defense, where the signatories agree to come to each other's aid in the event of an attack. Alliances are typically formed in response to perceived threats, allowing states to pool their military resources and strengthen their collective defense capabilities. The North Atlantic Treaty Organization (NATO) is one of the most well-known alliances, created during the Cold War to counter the threat posed by the Soviet Union. NATO's principle of collective defense, enshrined in Article 5 of its founding treaty, states that an attack on one member is considered an attack on all members, obligating them to respond collectively.

Alliances can be both bilateral and multilateral. Bilateral alliances involve two states, while multilateral alliances involve multiple states. The effectiveness of alliances depends on the strength of the commitments made by the member states and their willingness to uphold these commitments in times of crisis. However, alliances can also create tensions and rivalries, particularly if they are perceived as threatening by other states. The formation of opposing alliances can lead to an arms race and increase the risk of conflict, as seen in the lead-up to World War I.

Collective security, in contrast to alliances, is a broader concept that seeks to maintain peace and security through the cooperation of the entire international community. The idea behind collective security is that all states have a shared interest in preventing aggression and maintaining peace. **Under a collective security framework, states agree to collectively respond to any act of aggression, regardless of where it occurs or who the aggressor is.** The League of Nations, established after World War I, was an early attempt to implement collective security, although it ultimately failed to prevent the outbreak of World War II.

The United Nations (UN) represents the most significant effort to establish a global system of collective security. The UN Charter outlines the principles of collective security, with the UN Security Council playing a central role in maintaining international peace and security. **The Security Council has the authority to determine the existence of a threat to peace and to take collective action, including the use of force, to restore peace.** However, the effectiveness of the UN's collective security system has been limited by the veto power held by the five permanent members of the Security Council (China, France, Russia, the United Kingdom, and the United States). This power allows any one of these members to block collective action, even in the face of clear threats to international security.

While both alliances and collective security aim to enhance the security of states, they operate on different principles and scales. Alliances are based on specific mutual interests and commitments, often in response to particular threats. They are usually limited to a smaller group of states with shared security concerns. Collective security, on the other hand, is based on the idea of universal security, where all states have an interest in preventing aggression and maintaining peace. This broader approach seeks to create a more stable and peaceful international order by ensuring that acts of aggression are met with a unified response from the global community.

The success of alliances and collective security depends on the willingness of states to cooperate and uphold their commitments. Alliances require trust and a shared understanding of the threats they face, while collective security relies on the participation and cooperation of a broader range of states. In practice, both concepts face challenges, including the risk of alliance entanglement, the complexities of maintaining multilateral cooperation, and the influence of power politics on collective security efforts. Despite these challenges, alliances and collective security remain essential tools in the pursuit of international peace and stability.

In short, alliances and collective security are key mechanisms for maintaining international peace and security. Alliances provide a framework for states to cooperate on specific security issues, while collective security represents a broader approach to preventing aggression and maintaining global stability. Understanding the strengths and limitations of these concepts is crucial for navigating the complexities of international relations and ensuring a more peaceful world.

CHAPTER 7: THE GLOBAL ECONOMY AND INTERNATIONAL TRADE

Theories of International Trade

Theories of international trade provide the foundation for understanding why countries engage in trade, how they benefit from it, and what factors influence trade patterns. These theories have evolved over time, reflecting changes in economic thought and global realities.

Mercantilism is one of the earliest theories of international trade. Developed in the 16th to 18th centuries, mercantilism views trade as a zero-sum game where one nation's gain is another's loss. Mercantilists believed that a country should maximize its exports and minimize its imports to accumulate wealth, particularly in the form of gold and silver. **This led to policies such as high tariffs, colonial expansion, and the promotion of domestic industries to achieve a favorable balance of trade.** While mercantilism is largely discredited today, it laid the groundwork for the development of more sophisticated trade theories.

The theory of absolute advantage, introduced by Adam Smith in the late 18th century, challenged mercantilist ideas. Smith argued that trade is not a zero-sum game but can benefit all parties involved. According to Smith, a country has an absolute advantage if it can produce a good more efficiently than another country. In this scenario, each country should specialize in producing the goods for which it has an absolute advantage and then trade with others. This specialization and exchange would allow countries to consume more than they could produce on their own, leading to mutual benefits.

David Ricardo expanded on Smith's ideas with the theory of comparative advantage, which remains one of the most influential theories in international trade. Comparative advantage suggests that even if a country does not have an absolute advantage in producing any good, it can still benefit from trade by specializing in the production of goods for which it has the lowest opportunity cost. **In other words, a country should focus on producing the goods it can produce most efficiently, even if it is less efficient than other countries in producing those goods.** Trade allows countries to consume beyond their production possibilities, resulting in overall gains for all trading partners.

The Heckscher-Ohlin (H-O) model, developed in the early 20th century, further refines the theory of comparative advantage by focusing on a country's factor endowments—its relative abundance of labor, capital, and land. The H-O model argues that countries will export goods that require the factors of production they have in abundance and import goods that require factors they lack. **For example, a country with an abundance of capital but limited labor would specialize in capital-intensive goods and trade for labor-intensive goods.** This model highlights the role of resource endowments in shaping trade patterns and has been instrumental in explaining the trade dynamics between developed and developing countries.

In the 1980s, Paul Krugman introduced the New Trade Theory, which incorporates the concepts of economies of scale and network effects. Unlike traditional theories that assume constant returns to scale, New Trade Theory suggests that industries can experience increasing returns to scale, meaning that as production increases, the cost per unit decreases. This can lead to the concentration of certain industries in specific countries, not necessarily because of comparative advantage, but due to the benefits of large-scale production and access to larger markets. The theory also explains why countries with similar endowments and levels of development often trade similar goods—known as intra-industry trade—such as cars or electronics.

The theory of competitive advantage, introduced by Michael Porter, shifts the focus from factors of production to the role of innovation, technology, and firm strategy in shaping a country's trade patterns. Porter argues that countries gain a competitive advantage not just through their natural resources or labor force but by fostering industries that can innovate and improve productivity. Government policies, infrastructure, and the quality of institutions also play crucial roles in creating and sustaining competitive advantages in global markets. This theory emphasizes the importance of dynamic factors in maintaining a country's position in the global economy.

Finally, trade theories have also expanded to consider the impact of globalization and the rise of global value chains (GVCs). GVCs involve the fragmentation of production processes across different countries, where each country specializes in specific stages of production rather than entire goods.

These theories of international trade provide valuable insights into the mechanisms that drive global commerce. **They help explain why countries trade, what they trade, and how they benefit from trade.** As the global economy continues to evolve, these theories will remain essential tools for understanding and navigating the complexities of international trade.

Globalization and its Economic Impact

Globalization refers to the increasing interconnectedness and interdependence of the world's economies, cultures, and populations, driven by advances in communication, transportation, and technology. **Globalization has profoundly impacted the global economy, shaping trade, investment, labor markets, and**

economic development. Its effects are both positive and negative, varying across regions, industries, and social groups.

One of the most significant economic impacts of globalization is the expansion of international trade. As countries open their markets and reduce trade barriers, goods and services flow more freely across borders. This increase in trade has allowed countries to specialize in the production of goods and services for which they have a comparative advantage, leading to greater efficiency and higher overall economic output. For example, countries like China and India have become global manufacturing hubs, producing a wide range of goods at lower costs, which are then exported to markets around the world.

Globalization has also led to the growth of foreign direct investment (FDI). Multinational corporations (MNCs) expand their operations into new markets, seeking to capitalize on lower labor costs, access to resources, and new consumer bases. **FDI has been important in the economic development of many emerging markets, bringing in capital, technology, and expertise.** For instance, countries like Vietnam and Mexico have attracted significant FDI in manufacturing, boosting their economies and creating jobs.

However, the benefits of globalization are not evenly distributed. While globalization has lifted millions out of poverty, particularly in Asia, it has also led to significant economic disruptions in other regions. In advanced economies, globalization has contributed to the decline of certain industries, such as manufacturing in the United States and Europe, leading to job losses and wage stagnation for some workers. The competition from lower-cost producers abroad has put pressure on domestic industries, forcing companies to either innovate or relocate production to remain competitive.

Income inequality is another critical issue associated with globalization. While globalization has created wealth and opportunities, it has also widened the gap between the rich and the poor within and between countries. In many cases, the gains from globalization have been concentrated among the wealthiest individuals and multinational corporations, while lower-income workers and smaller businesses have faced increased competition and reduced bargaining power. This growing inequality has sparked debates about the fairness of globalization and calls for policies to ensure more equitable distribution of its benefits.

Globalization has also facilitated the spread of technology and innovation. As companies and countries interact more closely, they exchange ideas, knowledge, and technologies. **This diffusion of innovation has accelerated technological progress and productivity growth, contributing to economic development.** For example, advancements in information and communication technology (ICT) have enabled businesses to operate more efficiently and reach global markets, while also fostering innovation in sectors such as healthcare, finance, and education.

The integration of global financial markets is another significant aspect of globalization. Capital can now move more freely across borders, allowing investors to diversify their portfolios and companies to access financing from a global pool of capital. However, this increased financial interconnectedness also comes with risks, as financial crises can spread more easily from one country to another. The 2008 global financial crisis, which began in the United States, quickly impacted economies around the world, demonstrating how interconnected financial markets can amplify economic shocks.

Globalization has also influenced labor markets, both positively and negatively. On the positive side, globalization has created new job opportunities, particularly in emerging markets, where MNCs have set up operations. Workers in these countries have gained access to better-paying jobs, improved working conditions, and new skills. On the negative side, globalization has led to the outsourcing of jobs from higher-wage countries to lower-wage countries, contributing to job losses and wage pressure in some industries in developed economies. This has fueled concerns about job security and the erosion of labor standards.

Environmental impact is another important aspect of globalization. The increase in global trade and industrial production has led to higher levels of pollution, resource depletion, and environmental degradation. Globalization has also contributed to climate change, as the expansion of global supply chains and increased transportation have resulted in higher greenhouse gas emissions. On the other hand, globalization has facilitated international cooperation on environmental issues, leading to agreements such as the Paris Agreement on climate change.

Trade Agreements and Economic Integration

Trade agreements and economic integration are critical components of the global economy, shaping how countries interact and collaborate on trade and investment. These agreements range from bilateral deals between two countries to comprehensive regional agreements involving multiple nations. The primary goal of trade agreements is to reduce or eliminate barriers to trade, such as tariffs, quotas, and regulations, to promote economic growth and cooperation.

One of the most well-known types of trade agreements is the Free Trade Agreement (FTA). FTAs involve the reduction or elimination of tariffs and other trade barriers between the signatory countries, allowing for the freer flow of goods and services. The North American Free Trade Agreement (NAFTA), which was recently replaced by the United States-Mexico-Canada Agreement (USMCA), is a prominent example of an FTA. NAFTA significantly increased trade and investment between the United States, Canada, and Mexico, although it also sparked debates over its impact on jobs and industries in the participating countries.

Customs unions represent a deeper level of economic integration than FTAs. In a customs union, member countries agree to eliminate trade barriers among themselves and adopt a common external tariff on imports from non-member countries. The European Union (EU) began as a customs union, with member states benefiting from the free movement of goods within the union and a unified trade policy towards non-members. The EU's customs union has helped create a single market with significant economic benefits, but it has also required member states to cede some control over their trade policies to the EU.

Common markets go further than customs unions by allowing not only the free movement of goods but also the free movement of services, capital, and labor. The EU is also an example of a common market, where citizens of member states can live, work, and invest in any other member state without restrictions. This level of integration promotes greater economic efficiency and competition, leading to increased productivity and economic growth. However, it also requires significant coordination and harmonization of regulations, which can be challenging to achieve.

Economic unions represent the highest level of economic integration, where member states not only share a common market but also coordinate their economic policies and, in some cases, adopt a common currency. The EU's Economic and Monetary Union (EMU) is an example, with 19 of the 27 EU member states using the euro as their currency. The euro has facilitated trade and investment by eliminating exchange rate risks and reducing transaction costs within the eurozone. However, the EMU also poses challenges, as member states must align their fiscal and monetary policies, which can be difficult given their different economic conditions and priorities.

Bilateral trade agreements are another important tool for economic integration. These agreements involve two countries and typically focus on specific areas of trade and investment. **Bilateral agreements can be tailored to the unique needs and interests of the participating countries, allowing for more targeted and flexible arrangements.** For example, the Comprehensive Economic and Trade Agreement (CETA) between Canada and the EU eliminates most tariffs and provides greater access to each other's markets for goods, services, and investment.

Multilateral trade agreements, such as those negotiated under the World Trade Organization (WTO), involve multiple countries and aim to create a more open and predictable trading system. The WTO's agreements cover a wide range of issues, including tariffs, trade in services, intellectual property, and dispute resolution. While multilateral agreements can provide significant benefits by reducing trade barriers on a global scale, they are often challenging to negotiate due to the diverse interests of the participating countries.

Regional trade agreements (RTAs) are also common, involving countries within a specific geographic area. RTAs can range from FTAs and customs unions to more comprehensive arrangements like the EU. The Asia-Pacific Economic Cooperation (APEC) is an example of an RTA that promotes trade and investment in the Asia-Pacific region, although it does not involve the same level of integration as the EU. RTAs can enhance regional cooperation, but they can also create trade diversion, where trade shifts away from more efficient global producers to less efficient regional partners due to preferential treatment.

The Role of Multinational Corporations

Multinational corporations (MNCs) are companies that operate in multiple countries, often with a global presence in terms of production, marketing, and sales. **MNCs are important in the global economy, influencing trade, investment, and economic development.** Their operations and strategies have far-reaching implications for the countries in which they operate, as well as for the broader global economic system.

One of the primary ways MNCs impact the global economy is through foreign direct investment (FDI). MNCs invest in establishing or acquiring operations in foreign countries, such as factories, offices, and distribution networks. FDI by MNCs brings capital, technology, and expertise to host countries, contributing to economic growth and development. For example, MNCs in the automotive industry, like Toyota and Volkswagen, have established manufacturing plants in various countries, creating jobs, transferring technology, and integrating local economies into global supply chains.

MNCs also have key roles in global trade. They often operate complex global value chains (GVCs), where different stages of production are spread across multiple countries. This allows MNCs to take advantage of differences in labor costs, resources, and expertise, optimizing their production processes to reduce costs and increase efficiency. For instance, an MNC might design products in one country, manufacture components in another, and assemble the final product in yet another country before distributing it globally. This globalized production model has contributed to the growth of international trade and has increased the interconnectedness of economies.

MNCs can drive economic development in host countries by creating jobs, increasing productivity, and boosting exports. When MNCs establish operations in developing countries, they often provide access to better-paying jobs, training, and skills development. This can lead to higher productivity and improved living standards for local workers. Moreover, by integrating local firms into their supply chains, MNCs can help boost exports and increase the competitiveness of local industries. For example, the presence of technology giants like Intel and Microsoft in countries like India and Vietnam has spurred the growth of local IT industries and enhanced the global competitiveness of these countries.

However, the influence of MNCs is not without challenges and controversies. Critics argue that MNCs can exert significant influence over host countries, sometimes to the detriment of local economies and societies. MNCs may prioritize profits over social and environmental concerns, leading to negative outcomes such as labor exploitation, environmental degradation, and the erosion of local cultures. The collapse of the Rana Plaza garment factory in Bangladesh in 2013, where several MNCs were involved, highlighted the risks of poor labor practices in global supply chains.

MNCs also pose challenges to national sovereignty and economic policy. Their ability to move capital and operations across borders gives them leverage in negotiating favorable terms with host governments, such as tax incentives, relaxed regulations, or weak labor standards. This can lead to a "race to the bottom," where countries compete to attract MNCs by lowering regulatory standards, potentially undermining workers' rights, environmental protections, and public welfare. Additionally, the influence of MNCs in shaping global trade policies and agreements has raised concerns about the balance of power between corporations and governments.

Tax avoidance is another significant issue associated with MNCs. Many MNCs use complex legal structures and transfer pricing strategies to shift profits to low-tax jurisdictions, reducing their tax liabilities in higher-tax countries. This practice, known as base erosion and profit shifting (BEPS), deprives governments of significant tax revenues that could be used for public services and infrastructure. In response, international efforts, such as the OECD's BEPS initiative, have sought to address these challenges and ensure that MNCs pay their fair share of taxes.

Despite these challenges, MNCs also have the potential to drive positive change. As global actors, they can set standards for corporate social responsibility (CSR) and sustainability, influencing practices across their supply chains and industries. **Many MNCs have adopted CSR initiatives that focus on environmental sustainability, fair labor practices, and ethical sourcing.** For instance, companies like Unilever and Patagonia have committed to reducing their environmental footprint and improving the social impact of their operations, setting an example for others in their industries.

CHAPTER 8: INTERNATIONAL POLITICAL ECONOMY

Economic Theories in IR (Mercantilism, Liberalism, Marxism)

Economic theories in international relations provide different lenses through which we can understand the global economy and the interactions between states. Three major theories—mercantilism, liberalism, and Marxism—offer distinct perspectives on how economic power and wealth are distributed and used in the international system.

Mercantilism is one of the oldest economic theories in international relations. It emerged in the 16th century during the rise of European nation-states and is characterized by the belief that national power is directly linked to economic wealth. **Mercantilists argue that the state must actively manage the economy to increase national wealth, primarily through a favorable balance of trade.** This means exporting more than importing, accumulating gold and silver, and expanding overseas colonies to gain access to resources and markets. **Mercantilism views the global economy as a zero-sum game, where one state's gain is another's loss.** As a result, mercantilist policies often involve protectionism, such as tariffs and trade restrictions, to protect domestic industries from foreign competition.

Mercantilism is closely tied to the idea of economic nationalism, where states prioritize their own economic interests over those of others. **While the theory has largely been supplanted by more modern economic ideas, elements of mercantilism persist in contemporary policies, particularly in the form of trade protectionism and economic sanctions.** For example, tariffs imposed by governments to protect domestic industries or economic strategies aimed at achieving trade surpluses are reflections of mercantilist thinking.

Liberalism offers a stark contrast to mercantilism. Rooted in the ideas of classical economists like Adam Smith and David Ricardo, liberalism promotes free trade, open markets, and minimal government intervention in the economy. **Liberal theorists believe that individuals and states, acting in their self-interest, can achieve mutual benefits through trade and economic cooperation.** Unlike mercantilism, liberalism views the global economy as a positive-sum game, where all participants can gain from trade and exchange. This theory emphasizes the importance of comparative advantage, where each state should specialize in producing goods and services it can produce most efficiently, and then trade with others to maximize overall wealth.

Liberalism also supports the idea of international institutions and rules to facilitate cooperation and reduce the likelihood of conflict. **The establishment of** organizations like the World Trade Organization (WTO) and the International Monetary Fund (IMF) reflects liberal principles, aiming to create a stable and predictable international economic environment. These institutions promote free trade, investment, and the resolution of economic disputes, aligning with the liberal belief that open markets and economic interdependence contribute to global peace and prosperity.

Marxism offers a critical perspective on the global economy, focusing on the inequalities and power dynamics inherent in capitalism. Developed by Karl Marx in the 19th century, Marxism argues that the capitalist system is inherently exploitative, leading to the concentration of wealth and power in the hands of a few, while the majority are left in poverty. Marxists view the global economy as a system of class struggle, where the capitalist class (bourgeoisie) exploits the working class (proletariat) to maximize profits. This exploitation extends to the international level, where developed countries (the core) dominate and exploit developing countries (the periphery), creating a global division of labor that perpetuates inequality.

Marxism also critiques the idea of free markets, arguing that they do not lead to fair or efficient outcomes but rather to greater disparities in wealth and power. **In international relations, Marxist theory has been used to explain the persistence of poverty and underdevelopment in many parts of the world, attributing these issues to the global capitalist system.** Dependency theory, a derivative of Marxism, suggests that developing countries are kept in a state of dependency by the economic policies and practices of developed nations, which benefit from maintaining the status quo.

In contrast to liberalism's emphasis on cooperation and mutual benefit, Marxism views the global economy as inherently conflictual, driven by the interests of the powerful at the expense of the weak. **This perspective has influenced various movements and policies aimed at challenging the global capitalist order, from socialist revolutions to calls for a more equitable international economic system.**

Overall, these three economic theories—mercantilism, liberalism, and Marxism—offer distinct frameworks for understanding the complexities of international relations and the global economy. **Each theory highlights different aspects of how states interact economically, from the competitive and protectionist policies of mercantilism to the cooperative and market-oriented approach of liberalism, to the critical and conflict-driven analysis of Marxism.** Understanding these theories provides valuable insights into the motivations behind state behavior and the broader dynamics shaping the international economic system.

Globalization and Inequality

Globalization has profoundly shaped the global economy, creating new opportunities and challenges. **One of the most significant and contentious impacts of globalization is its effect on inequality, both within and between countries.** While globalization has driven economic growth and lifted millions out of poverty, it has also exacerbated disparities in income and wealth, leading to increased inequality.

Globalization has enabled the rapid expansion of international trade, investment, and technological innovation. These developments have fueled economic growth, particularly in emerging markets. **Countries like China, India, and Vietnam have experienced significant reductions in poverty and improvements in living standards due to their integration into the global economy.** However, the benefits of globalization have not been evenly distributed, and the gap between the rich and the poor has widened in many regions.

Within countries, globalization has often led to greater income inequality. In advanced economies, globalization has contributed to the decline of traditional manufacturing industries, as companies relocate production to countries with lower labor costs. **This has resulted in job losses and wage stagnation for low-skilled workers in developed countries, while high-skilled workers in sectors like technology and finance have seen their incomes rise.** The increased demand for skilled labor, driven by technological advances and global competition, has further widened the income gap between those with access to education and opportunities and those without.

In developing countries, globalization has created new economic opportunities but has also led to increased inequality. While some regions and sectors have benefited from foreign investment and access to global markets, others have been left behind. Rural areas, in particular, often lack the infrastructure and education needed to take advantage of globalization, leading to growing disparities between urban and rural populations. Additionally, the concentration of wealth in the hands of a few multinational corporations and elites has limited the broader distribution of globalization's benefits.

Globalization has also contributed to inequality between countries. While some developing countries have successfully integrated into the global economy and achieved rapid economic growth, others have struggled to compete. Countries with limited resources, poor infrastructure, and weak institutions have found it challenging to attract foreign investment or participate meaningfully in global trade. As a result, the income gap between rich and poor countries has widened, with many low-income countries remaining trapped in poverty despite the overall growth of the global economy.

The rise of global financial markets has further exacerbated inequality. The ability to move capital across borders has allowed wealthy individuals and corporations to maximize profits and minimize taxes, often at the expense of less mobile labor and small businesses. This has led to a concentration of wealth among the global elite, while ordinary workers and communities face increased economic insecurity. The global financial system, with its complex networks and speculative practices, has also contributed to financial crises that disproportionately affect the poor and vulnerable.

Addressing the inequality caused by globalization requires a multifaceted approach. Policies that promote inclusive growth, such as investment in education, infrastructure, and social safety nets, are essential for ensuring that the benefits of globalization are more widely shared. **International cooperation is also crucial for creating a fairer global economic system that reduces disparities between countries and within them.** By addressing the root causes of inequality, policymakers can help create a more equitable and sustainable global economy that benefits all.

The Role of International Financial Markets

International financial markets play an important part in the global economy, facilitating the flow of capital across borders, influencing exchange rates, and providing mechanisms for managing financial risks. **These markets encompass a wide range of financial instruments, including stocks, bonds, currencies, and derivatives, traded across various platforms and institutions worldwide.** The impact of international financial markets is profound, affecting everything from global economic growth to the financial stability of individual nations.

One of the primary functions of international financial markets is to allocate capital efficiently. By connecting investors with borrowers across different countries, these markets help channel funds to where they are most needed, promoting investment and economic growth. For instance, a company in a developing country might raise capital by issuing bonds or stocks in international markets, attracting investment from global investors who are seeking higher returns. This flow of capital can support infrastructure projects, business expansion, and technological innovation, contributing to economic development.

International financial markets also play a critical role in determining exchange rates. The foreign exchange market, or forex, is where currencies are traded, and exchange rates are determined based on supply and demand dynamics. **Exchange rates have a significant impact on international trade and investment, as they influence the relative prices of goods, services, and assets between countries.** A country with a strong currency may find its exports becoming more expensive and less competitive, while a weaker currency can boost export competitiveness but may lead to higher import costs and inflation.

Hedging and risk management are other essential functions of international financial markets. Companies and investors use various financial instruments, such as futures, options, and swaps, to protect themselves against fluctuations in exchange rates, interest rates, and commodity prices. **For example, an exporter might use currency futures to lock in an exchange rate for future sales, reducing the risk of currency depreciation.** Similarly, an investor might use interest rate swaps to manage the risk of fluctuating interest rates on their bond portfolio. These tools allow market participants to manage financial risks more effectively, providing greater stability and predictability in their operations.

International financial markets also influence global economic stability. On one hand, they provide a platform for diversification, allowing investors to spread their risks across different countries and asset classes. This diversification can reduce the impact of local economic downturns on global investors, contributing to overall financial stability. On the other hand, the interconnectedness of international financial markets means that financial crises can spread rapidly across borders, as seen during the global financial crisis of 2008. A crisis that begins in one country can quickly affect others through complex financial linkages, leading to global economic disruptions.

The role of international financial markets in shaping global economic policy is also significant. Central banks and governments closely monitor these markets to inform their monetary and fiscal policies. For example, movements in exchange rates can influence central banks' decisions on interest rates, while bond market trends can impact government borrowing costs and fiscal strategies. Additionally, international financial institutions like the International Monetary Fund (IMF) and the World Bank often intervene in financial markets to stabilize economies in crisis, providing loans and technical assistance to countries facing financial difficulties.

However, international financial markets also pose challenges and risks. The rapid movement of capital across borders, known as capital flows, can lead to economic volatility in both emerging and developed markets. Sudden surges of capital into a country can lead to asset bubbles and inflation, while abrupt outflows can trigger financial crises and currency collapses. The speculative nature of some financial markets, where investors seek short-term profits rather than long-term value, can exacerbate these risks, leading to economic instability and social unrest.

Regulation and oversight of international financial markets are crucial to mitigate these risks and ensure their smooth functioning. Governments and international organizations work together to establish rules and standards for financial markets, aiming to promote transparency, reduce systemic risks, and protect investors. The global financial regulatory framework includes institutions like the Basel Committee on Banking Supervision, which sets international banking standards, and the Financial Stability Board (FSB), which monitors and makes recommendations about the global financial system. These efforts are essential for maintaining the integrity and stability of international financial markets, especially in an increasingly interconnected and complex global economy.

Development and Poverty Alleviation

Development and poverty alleviation are central goals of international efforts to improve the quality of life for people in low-income countries. **These efforts focus on fostering economic growth, reducing inequality, and providing access to basic services such as education, healthcare, and clean water.** The challenges are complex and multifaceted, requiring coordinated action from governments, international organizations, and civil society.

Economic growth is often seen as a key driver of development and poverty alleviation. By increasing the overall wealth of a country, economic growth can create jobs, raise incomes, and improve living standards. However, growth alone is not enough; it must be inclusive and sustainable to have a lasting impact on poverty. This means ensuring that the benefits of growth are widely shared and that economic expansion does not come at the expense of environmental degradation or social inequality.

Investing in education and healthcare is critical for reducing poverty and promoting long-term development. Education empowers individuals with the skills and knowledge needed to participate in the economy and improve their livelihoods. Access to quality healthcare is equally important, as healthy populations are more productive and better able to contribute to economic growth. Programs that focus on improving education and healthcare outcomes, particularly for women and children, can have a significant impact on reducing poverty and fostering development.

Infrastructure development is another crucial aspect of poverty alleviation. Roads, bridges, and energy supplies are essential for connecting communities to markets, services, and opportunities. **In many low-income countries, inadequate infrastructure limits economic growth and exacerbates poverty by isolating rural areas and preventing access to essential services.** International development initiatives often prioritize infrastructure projects to stimulate economic activity and improve access to education, healthcare, and other basic services.

Social protection programs are vital for helping vulnerable populations escape poverty. These programs provide safety nets, such as cash transfers, food assistance, and unemployment benefits, to those who are most in need. By providing a basic level of income security, social protection helps to reduce poverty and inequality, especially during times of economic crisis or natural disasters. Well-designed social protection systems can also promote economic stability by supporting consumer demand and reducing the economic impact of shocks.

The role of international aid and development assistance is crucial in supporting poverty alleviation efforts in low-income countries. Foreign aid can provide much-needed resources for health, education, and infrastructure projects, as well as support for governance and institutional development. **However, the effectiveness of aid depends on how it is delivered and used.** Aid that is well-targeted and aligned with the needs and priorities of recipient countries can make a significant difference, while poorly managed aid can lead to dependency and corruption.

Microfinance and small-scale entrepreneurship have also emerged as important tools for poverty alleviation. Microfinance institutions provide small loans and financial services to individuals and small businesses that do not have access to traditional banking services. By enabling people to start or expand their businesses, microfinance can help lift them out of poverty and promote economic development at the grassroots level. Supporting small-scale entrepreneurship, particularly among women, can create jobs, increase incomes, and empower communities.

International trade can also have a role in poverty alleviation by opening up new markets and opportunities for low-income countries. By participating in global trade, developing countries can benefit from increased exports, investment, and technology transfer. However, trade must be fair and inclusive, with efforts to remove trade barriers and ensure that low-income countries can compete in the global marketplace. Trade policies that promote equitable access to markets and protect vulnerable industries are essential for ensuring that the benefits of trade contribute to poverty reduction.

Economic Sanctions and Their Political Impacts

Economic sanctions are a tool used by countries or international organizations to exert pressure on a state or entity to change its behavior. **Sanctions typically involve restricting trade, financial transactions, or access to resources, with the aim of achieving foreign policy objectives without resorting to military force.** While sanctions can be effective in certain contexts, they also have complex political impacts that can influence both the target country and the broader international community.

One of the primary goals of economic sanctions is to compel a change in behavior by the target country. This might involve stopping human rights abuses, ending a conflict, or halting the development of weapons of mass destruction. **Sanctions work by increasing the economic cost of the targeted actions,**

making it more difficult or expensive for the sanctioned country to continue
its behavior. For example, the United Nations imposed sanctions on Iraq in the
1990s to pressure the regime to dismantle its weapons programs. Similarly, the
United States and the European Union have used sanctions to pressure Iran to curb
its nuclear activities.

However, the effectiveness of sanctions in achieving their goals is often
debated. In some cases, sanctions have successfully pressured governments to
change course or come to the negotiating table. For example, international
sanctions played a role in bringing Iran to the negotiating table, leading to
the 2015 nuclear deal. In other cases, sanctions have failed to achieve their
objectives, either because the target country was able to find alternative economic
partners or because the political leadership was willing to endure economic
hardship rather than change its policies.

Sanctions can also have significant humanitarian impacts, often affecting the
civilian population of the target country more than the political elite.
Economic sanctions can lead to shortages of essential goods, inflation, and
unemployment, exacerbating poverty and suffering. For example, the sanctions on
Iraq in the 1990s led to widespread humanitarian crises, with severe shortages of
food and medicine. Critics argue that such outcomes undermine the moral
justification for sanctions and question their effectiveness in achieving political
goals.

The political impacts of sanctions extend beyond the target country.
Sanctions can strain diplomatic relations between the imposing country and other
states, particularly if they disagree with the sanctions or are economically affected
by them. For instance, U.S. sanctions on Cuba have long been a point of contention
in U.S.-Latin American relations, with many countries in the region opposing the
embargo. Similarly, sanctions on Russia following its annexation of Crimea in 2014
have led to tensions between Western countries and others that continue to do
business with Russia.

Sanctions can also influence domestic politics within the target country.
While the intended effect is to pressure the government, sanctions can sometimes
have the opposite effect, rallying public support around the leadership and fostering
a sense of nationalistic defiance. The Cuban government, for example, has used the
U.S. embargo as a rallying point to garner domestic support and blame economic
difficulties on foreign interference. Similarly, North Korea has used international
sanctions to justify its militaristic policies and maintain control over its population.

The use of sanctions as a political tool also raises questions about their
legality and ethics. International law allows for sanctions under specific
circumstances, such as when authorized by the United Nations Security Council.
However, unilateral sanctions, imposed without international consensus, are often
viewed as illegitimate or as violations of sovereignty. The ethical implications of

sanctions, particularly their humanitarian impact, are also widely debated, with critics arguing that they often harm the most vulnerable populations rather than the intended political targets.

Overall, economic sanctions are a powerful tool in international relations, capable of exerting significant pressure on target countries. However, their political impacts are complex and multifaceted, influencing not only the target country but also international relations and domestic politics. The effectiveness and ethical justification of sanctions remain subjects of debate, highlighting the need for careful consideration when using this tool to achieve foreign policy objectives.

CHAPTER 9: HUMAN RIGHTS AND HUMANITARIAN ISSUES

The Evolution of Human Rights in IR

The concept of human rights in international relations has evolved significantly over time, reflecting changing norms, political realities, and the growing recognition of the inherent dignity of all people. **The journey of human rights in international relations can be traced back to early philosophical ideas, but it gained concrete form and global attention primarily in the 20th century.**

The roots of human rights in international thought can be found in the Enlightenment era, where philosophers like John Locke and Jean-Jacques Rousseau emphasized the natural rights of individuals. These ideas influenced the American and French revolutions, embedding the notion that certain rights were inalienable and universal. However, these rights were initially understood within the context of state sovereignty and did not have a formal place in international relations.

The horrors of World War II marked a turning point in the evolution of human rights. The systematic atrocities committed during the war, particularly the Holocaust, shocked the global conscience and underscored the need for a universal framework to protect human rights. This led to the establishment of the United Nations in 1945, with one of its primary goals being the promotion and protection of human rights. The adoption of the Universal Declaration of Human Rights (UDHR) in 1948 was a landmark moment, as it articulated, for the first time, a comprehensive set of rights that were to be universally protected.

The UDHR, though not legally binding, set the stage for the development of international human rights law. It laid the groundwork for subsequent treaties and conventions that sought to codify these rights and make them enforceable. The International Covenant on Civil and Political Rights (ICCPR) and the International Covenant on Economic, Social, and Cultural Rights (ICESCR), both adopted in 1966, expanded on the rights outlined in the UDHR and created obligations for states to uphold them. Together, these documents form what is known as the International Bill of Human Rights.

Throughout the Cold War, human rights were often sidelined by the geopolitical tensions between the East and West. The Western bloc emphasized civil and political rights, while the Eastern bloc prioritized economic and social rights. This ideological divide limited the effectiveness of international human rights efforts, as each side accused the other of hypocrisy and failed to address human rights abuses within their own spheres of influence. However, human rights remained a significant issue, particularly as it became a tool for criticizing the other side's failures.

The end of the Cold War in the late 20th century brought a renewed focus on human rights in international relations. The collapse of the Soviet Union and the spread of democratic governance opened up new opportunities for advancing human rights globally. **International human rights organizations, such as Amnesty International and Human Rights Watch, gained prominence, and their advocacy efforts led to increased scrutiny of human rights practices worldwide.** The 1990s also saw the creation of international tribunals, such as those for the former Yugoslavia and Rwanda, which held individuals accountable for gross human rights violations, including genocide and crimes against humanity.

The concept of "humanitarian intervention" emerged during this period, reflecting the idea that the international community has a responsibility to protect populations from severe human rights abuses, even if it means violating state sovereignty. This principle, later formalized as the "Responsibility to Protect" (R2P), was endorsed by the UN in 2005. R2P asserts that the international community must intervene when a state is unable or unwilling to prevent mass atrocities within its borders, marking a significant shift in how human rights are addressed in international relations.

In recent years, human rights have become increasingly integrated into the broader framework of international relations. Human rights considerations now influence foreign policy, trade agreements, and international aid. Globalization and the rise of social media have also amplified the visibility of human rights issues, enabling activists and ordinary citizens to hold governments accountable for abuses. Despite these advancements, challenges remain, including the persistence of authoritarian regimes, the rise of populism, and the impact of global crises like the COVID-19 pandemic on human rights protections.

The evolution of human rights in international relations reflects a growing recognition that the protection of human dignity is not just a moral imperative but also a critical component of global peace and security. As international norms continue to evolve, the challenge will be to ensure that these rights are respected, protected, and fulfilled for all people, regardless of where they live.

Human Rights Violations and Global Responses

Human rights violations are severe breaches of fundamental rights and freedoms, often involving acts such as torture, arbitrary detention, discrimination, and extrajudicial killings. **These violations can occur in various contexts, including armed conflicts, authoritarian regimes, and even democratic societies where certain groups are marginalized.** The global community has developed a range of responses to address and prevent these violations, though the effectiveness of these responses varies.

One of the primary mechanisms for responding to human rights violations is through international law and treaties. The United Nations (UN) has established various conventions and protocols, such as the Convention Against Torture and the International Covenant on Civil and Political Rights, which oblige states to respect, protect, and fulfill human rights. When states ratify these treaties, they commit to upholding international human rights standards and are subject to periodic reviews by bodies like the UN Human Rights Council. However, the enforcement of these obligations often depends on the political will of states, and violations frequently go unpunished due to the complexities of international diplomacy.

Another critical response to human rights violations is the work of international human rights organizations. Groups like Amnesty International, Human Rights Watch, and the International Federation for Human Rights (FIDH) are important in documenting abuses, raising awareness, and advocating for justice. These organizations conduct investigations, publish reports, and engage in advocacy to hold perpetrators accountable and push for policy changes. Their efforts are vital in bringing attention to human rights violations that might otherwise be ignored or concealed by governments.

Global responses to human rights violations also include diplomatic pressure and sanctions. Countries and international organizations often use diplomatic channels to condemn human rights abuses and call for action. In some cases, economic sanctions, travel bans, and asset freezes are imposed on individuals, companies, or entire regimes responsible for severe human rights violations. For example, the international community has imposed sanctions on countries like North Korea, Iran, and Venezuela in response to their governments' human rights records. While sanctions can be effective in pressuring governments to change their behavior, they can also have unintended consequences, such as worsening the humanitarian situation for ordinary citizens.

The International Criminal Court (ICC) represents another avenue for addressing human rights violations, particularly those that constitute war crimes, genocide, and crimes against humanity. The ICC prosecutes individuals who are responsible for the most serious international crimes when national courts are unwilling or unable to do so. Since its establishment in 2002, the ICC has taken on several high-profile cases, bringing some perpetrators to justice and sending a message that impunity for human rights violations is unacceptable. However, the court's effectiveness is limited by its jurisdictional constraints and the reluctance of some countries to cooperate fully.

Global responses to human rights violations also involve humanitarian interventions, particularly in cases where mass atrocities are occurring. The international community, under the principle of the Responsibility to Protect (R2P), may intervene in a state's affairs to prevent or stop widespread human rights abuses. **This can include military intervention, as seen in the NATO-led intervention in Libya in 2011, or non-military actions such as diplomatic efforts and economic sanctions.** However, humanitarian interventions are controversial and often debated, particularly regarding their legality, effectiveness, and potential for abuse.

Despite these efforts, significant challenges remain in addressing human rights violations globally. **Political considerations often influence the response to human rights abuses, leading to selective enforcement or inaction in certain cases.** Additionally, the rise of authoritarianism and populism in various parts of the world has led to a backlash against international human rights norms, making it more difficult to address violations effectively. Nevertheless, the global commitment to human rights remains a powerful force, driven by the belief that all people deserve to live with dignity, freedom, and justice.

The Role of International Humanitarian Organizations

International humanitarian organizations play a vital role in responding to crises and providing assistance to those affected by conflicts, natural disasters, and other emergencies. **These organizations operate across borders, offering support in situations where local governments are either unable or unwilling to meet the needs of their populations.** Their work is guided by principles of humanity, neutrality, impartiality, and independence, ensuring that aid reaches those who need it most, regardless of political considerations.

One of the most prominent international humanitarian organizations is the International Committee of the Red Cross (ICRC). The ICRC is known for its work in conflict zones, where it provides medical care, food, and shelter to victims of war, and works to ensure the protection of civilians and prisoners of war under international humanitarian law. **The ICRC's mandate, based on the Geneva Conventions, allows it to operate in some of the world's most dangerous environments, offering critical services that often save lives.**

The United Nations Office for the Coordination of Humanitarian Affairs (OCHA) is another key player in the international humanitarian landscape. OCHA coordinates the global response to emergencies, bringing together UN agencies, NGOs, and other stakeholders to deliver aid effectively and efficiently. By facilitating collaboration and information sharing, OCHA ensures that resources are allocated where they are most needed and that humanitarian efforts are not duplicated or wasted.

Non-governmental organizations (NGOs) also are important in humanitarian efforts. Organizations like Médecins Sans Frontières (Doctors Without Borders), Save the Children, and CARE operate worldwide, providing medical care, education, food security, and other essential services in crisis situations. **These NGOs often work on the ground in areas where access is difficult, bringing specialized expertise and a commitment to helping vulnerable populations.** Their work is often supported by donations from individuals and governments, reflecting the global recognition of the importance of humanitarian aid.

Humanitarian organizations also advocate for the protection of human rights and the enforcement of international humanitarian law. They raise awareness of the conditions faced by people in crisis situations and pressure governments and international bodies to take action. For example, organizations like Amnesty International and Human Rights Watch document human rights abuses in conflict zones, providing evidence that can be used to hold perpetrators accountable and push for policy changes.

The work of international humanitarian organizations is not without challenges. They often operate in complex and dangerous environments where access to affected populations is restricted by security concerns, political obstacles, or logistical difficulties. These organizations must navigate the delicate balance between providing aid and maintaining neutrality, ensuring that their work is not co-opted by political agendas. Additionally, funding constraints and donor fatigue can limit their ability to respond to all crises, forcing difficult decisions about where to allocate resources.

Despite these challenges, international humanitarian organizations remain a critical component of the global response to crises. Their efforts provide a lifeline to millions of people each year, helping to alleviate suffering and rebuild communities affected by conflict, disaster, and other emergencies. Through their work, these organizations embody the principles of global solidarity and compassion, demonstrating the importance of collective action in addressing the world's most pressing humanitarian challenges.

Humanitarian Intervention and the Responsibility to Protect (R2P)

Humanitarian intervention and the Responsibility to Protect (R2P) are concepts rooted in the idea that the international community has an obligation to protect populations from mass atrocities when their own governments are unable or unwilling to do so. **These concepts have evolved in response to the failures of the international community to prevent or stop genocides and other large-scale human rights violations in the 20th century.**

Humanitarian intervention refers to the use of force by one or more states, or an international organization, to prevent or end gross human rights violations in another state, especially when the state in question is perpetrating the abuses. This idea gained prominence after the Rwandan Genocide in 1994 and the mass atrocities in the Balkans, where the international community was criticized for failing to act. Humanitarian intervention is controversial because it involves violating a state's sovereignty, a core principle of international law, in the name of protecting human rights.

The concept of R2P emerged in the early 2000s as a framework for addressing the limitations and controversies of humanitarian intervention. Endorsed by the United Nations in 2005, R2P is based on three pillars: the responsibility of the state to protect its populations from genocide, war crimes, ethnic cleansing, and crimes against humanity; the international community's responsibility to assist states in fulfilling this duty; and the responsibility of the international community to intervene, including with military force, when a state is failing to protect its population.

R2P represents a significant shift in how the international community approaches sovereignty and human rights. It posits that sovereignty is not just a right but a responsibility, and that the protection of populations from mass atrocities is a legitimate concern of the international community. The principle of R2P has been invoked in various contexts, including the international response to the crisis in Libya in 2011, where a NATO-led coalition intervened to protect civilians from the Gaddafi regime.

However, the implementation of R2P is fraught with challenges and criticisms. Critics argue that R2P can be misused as a pretext for advancing geopolitical interests under the guise of humanitarianism. For instance, the intervention in Libya has been criticized for going beyond the mandate to protect civilians and contributing to the country's subsequent instability. Additionally, there is often disagreement among international actors about when and how to apply R2P, leading to inconsistent responses and, at times, inaction in the face of atrocities, as seen in the ongoing conflicts in Syria and Yemen.

Despite these challenges, R2P remains a critical framework for addressing the most severe human rights violations. It underscores the idea that the international community cannot stand by while mass atrocities occur and that there is a collective responsibility to prevent and stop such crimes. The effectiveness of R2P depends on the political will of the international community, the ability to coordinate multilateral actions, and the commitment to upholding human rights without exploiting the concept for other purposes.

Overall, umanitarian intervention and R2P are powerful concepts in the international community's efforts to protect human rights, but their success relies on careful, principled application and genuine commitment to the welfare of affected populations. The challenge moving forward is to refine these concepts and their implementation to better balance the protection of human rights with respect for state sovereignty and to ensure that interventions genuinely serve the interests of those they are intended to protect.

CHAPTER 10: ENVIRONMENTAL ISSUES IN INTERNATIONAL RELATIONS

Climate Change and Global Environmental Policies

Climate change is one of the most pressing issues in international relations today, influencing global security, economic stability, and environmental sustainability. **The growing concentration of greenhouse gases in the atmosphere, primarily due to human activities like burning fossil fuels and deforestation, is causing global temperatures to rise.** This warming leads to severe consequences, including more frequent and intense natural disasters, rising sea levels, and disruptions to food and water supplies. **Addressing climate change requires coordinated global action, making it a central focus of international environmental policies.**

The international community has developed several key frameworks to combat climate change. The most significant is the United Nations Framework Convention on Climate Change (UNFCCC), established at the Earth Summit in Rio de Janeiro in 1992. The UNFCCC serves as the foundation for global climate negotiations, aiming to stabilize greenhouse gas concentrations at a level that would prevent dangerous interference with the climate system. The Convention has been pivotal in raising awareness about climate change and facilitating dialogue among nations.

Building on the UNFCCC, the Kyoto Protocol was adopted in 1997 as the first binding international agreement to reduce greenhouse gas emissions. The Protocol set specific targets for industrialized countries to cut their emissions, reflecting the principle of "common but differentiated responsibilities." This principle acknowledges that while all countries contribute to global emissions, developed nations bear a greater historical responsibility and have more resources to address the problem. However, the Kyoto Protocol faced challenges, including the withdrawal of key countries like the United States and the lack of binding commitments for developing nations, which limited its overall effectiveness.

The Paris Agreement, adopted in 2015, represents a more inclusive and flexible approach to global climate governance. Unlike the Kyoto Protocol, the Paris Agreement involves both developed and developing countries in the effort to combat climate change. It aims to limit global warming to well below 2 degrees Celsius above pre-industrial levels, with an aspirational target of 1.5 degrees Celsius. To achieve this, countries submit nationally determined contributions (NDCs), which outline their plans for reducing emissions and adapting to climate impacts. The Paris Agreement also emphasizes the importance of transparency and accountability, requiring countries to regularly report on their progress and update their NDCs every five years.

One of the key challenges in implementing global environmental policies is balancing economic growth with environmental protection. Developing countries often face the dilemma of needing to expand their economies and reduce poverty while also reducing emissions and protecting their natural resources. To address this, the Paris Agreement includes provisions for financial and technical support to help developing nations transition to low-carbon economies. The Green Climate Fund, established under the UNFCCC, is one mechanism for channeling financial resources to support climate action in developing countries, aiming to mobilize $100 billion annually by 2020.

Another critical aspect of global environmental policies is adaptation to the impacts of climate change. Even with significant efforts to reduce emissions, the effects of climate change are already being felt, particularly in vulnerable regions like small island states and sub-Saharan Africa. Adaptation involves measures to protect communities and ecosystems from the adverse effects of climate change, such as building resilient infrastructure, improving water management, and developing early warning systems for natural disasters. International cooperation is essential for sharing knowledge, technologies, and resources to enhance global adaptation efforts.

The role of non-state actors, including cities, businesses, and civil society, has become increasingly important in global climate governance. These actors are often at the forefront of innovation and implementation, driving progress even when national governments are slow to act. For example, many cities around the world have committed to ambitious climate goals, such as becoming carbon-neutral by mid-century. Similarly, businesses are investing in renewable energy, improving energy efficiency, and developing new technologies to reduce their carbon footprints.

Global environmental policies also face significant political challenges. Differences in national interests, economic priorities, and levels of development can hinder international cooperation. For instance, some countries rely heavily on fossil fuels for their economic growth and are reluctant to commit to stringent emission reductions. Additionally, geopolitical tensions can influence climate negotiations, as seen in the varying levels of commitment among major emitters like the United States, China, and the European Union.

International Environmental Agreements

International environmental agreements are essential tools in addressing global environmental challenges, such as climate change, biodiversity loss, and pollution.

These agreements bring together countries to collaborate on protecting the environment, setting standards, and implementing measures to mitigate environmental harm. Over the years, several key agreements have been established, shaping the global approach to environmental governance.

One of the earliest and most influential international environmental agreements is the 1972 Stockholm Declaration. This declaration, adopted at the United Nations Conference on the Human Environment in Stockholm, marked the beginning of global environmental diplomacy. The conference highlighted the interconnectedness of environmental issues and human development, leading to the creation of the United Nations Environment Programme (UNEP). The Stockholm Declaration laid the foundation for future environmental agreements by emphasizing the need for international cooperation in addressing environmental challenges.

The Montreal Protocol on Substances that Deplete the Ozone Layer, adopted in 1987, is another landmark international environmental agreement. The protocol was established in response to the discovery of the ozone hole over Antarctica, caused by the release of chlorofluorocarbons (CFCs) and other ozone-depleting substances. The Montreal Protocol is widely regarded as one of the most successful environmental treaties, as it has led to the phasing out of nearly 99% of ozone-depleting substances. The protocol's success demonstrates the effectiveness of international cooperation in addressing a specific environmental problem, with significant global benefits.

The Convention on Biological Diversity (CBD), adopted in 1992, is a key international agreement aimed at protecting biodiversity. The CBD was one of the three major agreements signed at the Rio Earth Summit, alongside the UN Framework Convention on Climate Change (UNFCCC) and the UN Convention to Combat Desertification (UNCCD). The CBD focuses on the conservation of biological diversity, the sustainable use of its components, and the fair and equitable sharing of benefits arising from genetic resources. The convention has been instrumental in promoting the protection of ecosystems, species, and genetic diversity, though challenges remain in its implementation.

The Paris Agreement, adopted in 2015 under the UNFCCC, represents a significant milestone in global efforts to combat climate change. Unlike its predecessor, the Kyoto Protocol, which set binding targets for developed countries, the Paris Agreement involves all countries in the fight against climate change. **The agreement aims to limit global warming to well below 2 degrees Celsius above pre-industrial levels, with an aspirational target of 1.5 degrees Celsius.** Countries submit nationally determined contributions (NDCs), outlining their plans for reducing greenhouse gas emissions and adapting to climate impacts. The Paris Agreement also emphasizes transparency, accountability, and the need for financial support to help developing countries transition to low-carbon economies.

In addition to these major agreements, there are numerous other international environmental treaties and conventions addressing specific issues. For example, the Basel Convention regulates the transboundary movements of hazardous wastes and their disposal, while the Ramsar Convention focuses on the conservation and sustainable use of wetlands. These agreements reflect the diversity of environmental challenges and the need for targeted, coordinated action at the international level.

Despite the progress made through international environmental agreements, challenges remain. Effective implementation and enforcement of these agreements require strong political will, adequate funding, and robust monitoring mechanisms. Moreover, balancing the interests of developed and developing countries is often a complex task, as economic development and environmental protection are sometimes seen as conflicting goals. Nevertheless, international environmental agreements remain crucial in the global effort to protect the planet and ensure a sustainable future.

Sustainable Development in IR

Sustainable development is a key concept in international relations, focusing on the need to balance economic growth, social inclusion, and environmental protection. This approach recognizes that development must meet the needs of the present without compromising the ability of future generations to meet their own needs. As global challenges like climate change, resource depletion, and social inequality intensify, sustainable development has become central to the international agenda.

The concept of sustainable development gained prominence with the 1987 Brundtland Report, formally titled "Our Common Future." The report, published by the World Commission on Environment and Development, defined sustainable development and emphasized the interconnectedness of environmental, economic, and social issues. This report laid the groundwork for integrating sustainability into international policies and agreements, influencing subsequent global initiatives.

The 1992 Rio Earth Summit marked a significant step in embedding sustainable development into international relations. The summit resulted in the adoption of Agenda 21, a comprehensive action plan for sustainable development at the global, national, and local levels. The Rio Declaration on Environment and Development, also adopted at the summit, outlined 27 principles to guide sustainable development, including the precautionary approach, the polluter pays principle, and the right to development. These principles have since become fundamental in shaping international environmental policies and agreements.

The Millennium Development Goals (MDGs), adopted in 2000, further integrated sustainable development into the global agenda. The MDGs set specific targets for reducing poverty, improving health and education, promoting gender equality, and ensuring environmental sustainability by 2015. **While progress was made in several areas, the MDGs highlighted the need for a more comprehensive and inclusive approach to development.** This realization led to the development of the Sustainable Development Goals (SDGs), which were adopted in 2015 as part of the 2030 Agenda for Sustainable Development.

The SDGs represent a universal call to action to end poverty, protect the planet, and ensure prosperity for all. Comprising 17 goals and 169 targets, the SDGs address a wide range of issues, from climate action and clean energy to quality education and reduced inequalities. The SDGs emphasize the need for a holistic approach to development, recognizing that progress in one area often depends on advancements in others. For example, achieving food security (Goal 2) is closely linked to sustainable agricultural practices (Goal 12), access to clean water (Goal 6), and climate resilience (Goal 13).

International relations is important in advancing sustainable development, as global challenges require coordinated efforts and shared responsibilities. Multilateral institutions like the United Nations, the World Bank, and the International Monetary Fund (IMF) are key actors in promoting sustainable development through policy guidance, financial support, and capacity-building initiatives. These institutions work with governments, civil society, and the private sector to implement sustainable development strategies that align with global goals and local contexts.

Trade and investment are also important components of sustainable development in international relations. The challenge is to ensure that economic activities contribute to sustainable outcomes, rather than exacerbating environmental degradation or social inequalities. For example, international trade agreements increasingly include provisions on labor rights, environmental standards, and sustainable resource management, reflecting the growing recognition of the need to integrate sustainability into global economic practices.

Despite significant progress, achieving sustainable development remains a complex and ongoing challenge. Conflicting interests between economic growth and environmental protection, as well as the uneven distribution of resources and opportunities, complicate efforts to implement sustainable development globally. **Nevertheless, the commitment to sustainable development continues to shape international relations, driving efforts to create a more just, equitable, and sustainable world for all.**

The Politics of Natural Resources

The politics of natural resources is a critical aspect of international relations, shaping the dynamics between states and influencing global security, economic development, and environmental sustainability. **Natural resources, such as oil, gas, minerals, water, and forests, are vital to the economic and social well-being of nations, but their uneven distribution across the globe often leads to competition, conflict, and complex geopolitical strategies.**

Oil and gas are among the most strategically important natural resources, and their control has been a central focus of international politics for decades. The Middle East, home to some of the world's largest oil reserves, has been a region of intense geopolitical interest, with major powers vying for influence and control over these resources. Countries that are rich in oil and gas often hold significant leverage in global politics, as seen with the Organization of the Petroleum Exporting Countries (OPEC), which has the ability to influence global oil prices by adjusting production levels. This leverage can lead to alliances, but it can also spark conflicts, as seen in the Gulf Wars, where control over oil resources played a key role.

The competition for natural resources is not limited to oil and gas. Minerals, such as rare earth elements, are essential for modern technologies, including smartphones, electric vehicles, and military hardware. **China, which controls a significant portion of the world's rare earth production, has used this dominance as a strategic tool in its international relations, occasionally restricting exports to exert pressure on other countries.** This has prompted efforts by other nations to diversify their supply chains and reduce dependence on Chinese rare earths, leading to geopolitical tensions.

Water is another critical natural resource with significant political implications. Unlike oil and minerals, water is essential for life, and its scarcity can lead to severe conflicts, especially in regions where water resources cross national borders. The Nile River, for example, flows through several countries in northeastern Africa, including Ethiopia, Sudan, and Egypt. Disputes over the allocation and use of the Nile's waters have led to long-standing tensions, particularly between Egypt, which relies heavily on the river for its water supply, and Ethiopia, which is developing the Grand Ethiopian Renaissance Dam (GERD) to generate hydroelectric power. These disputes underscore the complexities of managing shared natural resources, where the needs and interests of multiple countries must be balanced.

Forests and other renewable resources also are important in international politics. The Amazon Rainforest, often referred to as the "lungs of the Earth," is critical for global biodiversity and climate regulation. However, deforestation driven by agricultural expansion, logging, and infrastructure development in countries like Brazil has become a contentious issue in international relations. While Brazil argues that it has the sovereign right to develop its natural resources, the international community, particularly environmental organizations and other governments, has expressed concern about the global impact of Amazon deforestation on climate change and biodiversity loss. This tension between national sovereignty and global environmental responsibility highlights the challenges of managing natural resources in a way that balances local and global interests.

The politics of natural resources is also closely linked to economic development and poverty alleviation. For many developing countries, natural resources are a primary source of income and a key driver of economic growth. However, the phenomenon known as the "resource curse" suggests that countries rich in natural resources often experience slower economic growth, higher levels of corruption, and greater political instability compared to resource-poor countries. This paradox occurs because resource wealth can lead to mismanagement, dependency on volatile global markets, and neglect of other sectors of the economy. To address the resource curse, some countries have implemented measures such as the establishment of sovereign wealth funds, which invest resource revenues in diversified assets to promote long-term economic stability.

Environmental concerns are increasingly influencing the politics of natural resources. As the world grapples with climate change and environmental degradation, there is growing pressure on countries to manage their natural resources sustainably. This shift is evident in the global push towards renewable energy, where countries are investing in wind, solar, and other renewable resources to reduce their dependence on fossil fuels and mitigate the impacts of climate change. However, the transition to renewable energy also involves geopolitical considerations, as it alters the balance of power between resource-rich and resource-poor countries and raises questions about access to critical minerals needed for renewable technologies.

Transboundary Environmental Issues (e.g., Water Sharing, Air Pollution)

Transboundary environmental issues, such as water sharing and air pollution, present significant challenges in international relations because they require cooperation across national borders. **These issues arise when environmental resources or pollutants cross boundaries, affecting multiple countries and necessitating joint efforts to manage or mitigate their impact.** Addressing these challenges is important for maintaining regional stability, protecting public health, and ensuring the sustainable use of shared resources.

Water sharing is one of the most contentious transboundary environmental issues. Rivers, lakes, and aquifers often cross national borders, leading to disputes over the allocation and use of water resources. **The Nile River, which flows through eleven countries in northeastern Africa, is a prime example of the**

complexities involved in transboundary water management. Countries like Egypt, Sudan, and Ethiopia have competing interests in the Nile's waters, with Egypt relying heavily on the river for its water supply, while Ethiopia seeks to use the river for hydroelectric power generation. The construction of the Grand Ethiopian Renaissance Dam (GERD) has heightened tensions between these countries, highlighting the need for effective international agreements to manage shared water resources.

The Indus River Basin, shared by India and Pakistan, is another example of the challenges posed by transboundary water issues. The Indus Waters Treaty, signed in 1960, has helped manage water distribution between the two countries for decades, even during periods of political tension. However, climate change, population growth, and increasing water demand are putting additional pressure on the basin, raising concerns about the long-term sustainability of the treaty. Effective transboundary water management requires continuous dialogue, trust-building, and the willingness of countries to cooperate on shared water resources, even in the face of broader political disputes.

Air pollution is another major transboundary environmental issue, with pollutants like smog, particulate matter, and greenhouse gases traveling across borders and affecting multiple countries. One of the most well-known examples of transboundary air pollution is acid rain, which occurs when sulfur dioxide ($SO2$) and nitrogen oxides (NOx) emitted by industrial activities combine with atmospheric moisture and fall as acidic precipitation. In the 1980s, acid rain caused significant environmental damage in Europe and North America, leading to the negotiation of international agreements such as the 1979 Convention on Long-Range Transboundary Air Pollution (CLRTAP). This convention, which was the first international agreement to address air pollution on a broad regional scale, has been instrumental in reducing emissions of sulfur and nitrogen compounds and mitigating the impacts of acid rain.

Another example of transboundary air pollution is the haze that frequently affects Southeast Asia, caused by forest fires in Indonesia. The haze, which often blankets neighboring countries like Malaysia and Singapore, poses serious health risks and has economic impacts due to reduced visibility and disruptions to transportation and tourism. Despite regional agreements such as the ASEAN Agreement on Transboundary Haze Pollution, addressing the root causes of the haze, such as illegal land clearing and weak enforcement of environmental laws, remains a significant challenge. The issue highlights the difficulties in achieving effective regional cooperation when national interests and enforcement capacities vary widely.

Climate change is a global transboundary issue that affects every country, but its impacts are felt most acutely in vulnerable regions like small island states and low-lying coastal areas. Greenhouse gases emitted by one country contribute to global warming, which in turn leads to rising sea levels, more frequent extreme weather events, and disruptions to food and water supplies worldwide. Addressing climate change requires a coordinated international response, as exemplified by the Paris Agreement, which aims to limit global temperature rise and reduce greenhouse gas emissions through nationally determined contributions (NDCs). However, the varying capacities and commitments of countries to reduce emissions and adapt to climate impacts present ongoing challenges for global cooperation.

CHAPTER 11: REGIONAL CONFLICTS AND GLOBAL IMPACTS

The Middle East and International Politics

The Middle East plays a central role in international politics, influenced by its strategic location, vast energy resources, and complex historical and religious dynamics. **This region has been a focal point of global power struggles, with major international actors vying for influence, often through both direct intervention and indirect means.**

Oil has been a driving factor in the Middle East's significance in international relations. The region holds a significant portion of the world's proven oil reserves, making it a critical supplier of energy to global markets. Countries like Saudi Arabia, Iraq, and Iran have used their oil wealth to exert influence both regionally and globally. The control of oil resources has often been linked to power struggles, as seen in the geopolitical tensions surrounding the Strait of Hormuz, a vital chokepoint through which a large percentage of the world's oil supply passes. The 1973 oil embargo by OPEC, led by Middle Eastern countries, demonstrated the region's ability to influence global economics and politics. The embargo led to severe economic disruptions in the West, illustrating how deeply interconnected the Middle East is with global energy security.

The Arab-Israeli conflict has also been a major factor in shaping international politics in the Middle East. The establishment of Israel in 1948 and the subsequent wars with its Arab neighbors have had lasting impacts on the region. This conflict has drawn in major powers, including the United States, which has been a staunch ally of Israel, and the Soviet Union, which historically supported Arab states. The ongoing Israeli-Palestinian conflict remains a source of instability, with various international efforts to mediate peace often resulting in temporary solutions rather than lasting resolutions. The conflict continues to affect regional alliances, with some Arab states normalizing relations with Israel in recent years under the Abraham Accords, while others maintain their opposition.

Religious and sectarian divides further complicate the political landscape of the Middle East. The Sunni-Shia divide, most prominently represented by the rivalry between Saudi Arabia and Iran, influences many of the region's conflicts. **This sectarian rivalry has played out in various proxy wars, such as in Yemen, Syria, and Iraq, where both Saudi Arabia and Iran support opposing factions.** These conflicts have not only destabilized the region but have also drawn in international powers, each seeking to support their regional allies while countering the influence of their rivals.

The United States has had a particularly influential role in the Middle East, driven by its strategic interests in securing oil supplies, combating terrorism, and supporting allies like Israel and Saudi Arabia. U.S. involvement has included military interventions, such as the Gulf War in 1991, which was aimed at expelling Iraqi forces from Kuwait, and the 2003 invasion of Iraq, justified by the controversial claims of weapons of mass destruction. These interventions have had far-reaching consequences, including the destabilization of Iraq, the rise of insurgent groups like ISIS, and a broader questioning of U.S. foreign policy in the region.

Russia has also sought to expand its influence in the Middle East, particularly in recent years. Moscow's support for the Assad regime in Syria has been a key element of its strategy to reassert itself as a major power in the region. By intervening in the Syrian civil war, Russia has secured a foothold in the Eastern Mediterranean and positioned itself as a crucial player in any future political settlement. This intervention has complicated U.S. and Western efforts to influence the outcome of the Syrian conflict and has highlighted the growing multipolarity in Middle Eastern politics.

The Middle East is also a significant arena for global power competition beyond the U.S.-Russia dynamic. China, for example, has been steadily increasing its presence in the region through economic investments, particularly under its Belt and Road Initiative (BRI). **China's approach has focused on economic rather than military engagement, seeking to secure energy supplies and expand its influence through infrastructure projects and trade.** This growing involvement adds another layer of complexity to the region's already intricate web of alliances and rivalries.

Terrorism and extremism originating from the Middle East have also had profound global impacts. Groups like Al-Qaeda and ISIS have not only destabilized the region but have also carried out attacks around the world, prompting international counterterrorism efforts. These groups have exploited the region's conflicts and instability to recruit fighters and expand their influence, leading to military interventions, intelligence operations, and diplomatic initiatives aimed at countering their threat.

The Middle East remains a region where local conflicts can quickly escalate into broader international crises. The interplay of religious, ethnic, and geopolitical factors, combined with the involvement of major global powers, makes it one of the most complex and volatile areas in the world. As such, the Middle East will likely continue to be a central focus of international politics, with its developments having significant implications for global security, energy markets, and diplomatic relations.

Asian Geopolitics and Power Struggles

Asian geopolitics is characterized by a complex interplay of power struggles, regional rivalries, and strategic alliances. **The region's vast size, diverse cultures, and varying levels of economic development contribute to its geopolitical significance.** Major powers like China, India, Japan, and Russia, along with the United States' strategic interests, have important roles in shaping the dynamics of the region.

China's rise as a global power is one of the most significant factors influencing Asian geopolitics. Over the past few decades, China has transformed its economy and expanded its influence across Asia and beyond. Through its Belt and Road Initiative (BRI), China has invested in infrastructure projects in numerous countries, extending its economic and political reach. While these investments offer development opportunities, they also create dependencies that China can leverage for strategic purposes. This growing influence has led to concerns among neighboring countries and has prompted a strategic response, particularly from the United States, which seeks to counterbalance China's assertiveness.

The South China Sea is a major flashpoint in Asia, reflecting the broader power struggle between China and other regional actors. China claims nearly the entire South China Sea, through which a significant portion of global trade passes, based on its controversial "nine-dash line." This claim is contested by several Southeast Asian nations, including Vietnam, the Philippines, and Malaysia, all of which have overlapping territorial claims. China has reinforced its claims by building artificial islands and militarizing the area, leading to increased tensions and occasional confrontations. The United States, while not a claimant, has conducted freedom of navigation operations in the region, emphasizing the importance of maintaining open sea lanes and challenging China's expansive claims.

India, another major power in Asia, is both a competitor and a counterbalance to China. The two countries share a long, disputed border, which has been the site of multiple conflicts, including the brief but bloody 1962 Sino-Indian War and more recent skirmishes in the Himalayas. India views China's rise with caution, particularly given China's growing influence in South Asia through investments in Pakistan, Sri Lanka, and Nepal. In response, India has sought to strengthen its own regional influence and has engaged in strategic partnerships with countries like Japan, Australia, and the United States, as seen in the Quadrilateral Security Dialogue (Quad). The Quad, often viewed as a counterbalance to China, focuses on promoting a free and open Indo-Pacific region, with an emphasis on maritime security, economic cooperation, and infrastructure development.

Japan's role in Asian geopolitics is shaped by its economic strength and its alliance with the United States. As the world's third-largest economy, Japan has significant influence in regional trade and investment. However, Japan's security posture has been constrained by its pacifist constitution, which limits its military capabilities. Despite these constraints, Japan has taken steps to enhance its security role in Asia, including expanding its Self-Defense Forces and increasing defense cooperation with the United States and other regional partners. Japan is particularly concerned about China's military assertiveness and North Korea's nuclear and missile programs, both of which pose direct threats to Japanese security.

Russia, while geographically straddling both Europe and Asia, plays a strategic role in Asian geopolitics, particularly in Northeast Asia and Central Asia. Russia's interests in Asia are driven by its need to secure its eastern borders, maintain influence in former Soviet republics, and counterbalance U.S. and Chinese power. In Northeast Asia, Russia has sought to strengthen its ties with China, particularly in the areas of energy and defense, while also maintaining a complex relationship with Japan, marked by the unresolved Kuril Islands dispute. In Central Asia, Russia views the region as part of its traditional sphere of influence and has sought to counter Chinese economic penetration through initiatives like the Eurasian Economic Union.

The Korean Peninsula remains a focal point of tension in Asian geopolitics, particularly due to North Korea's nuclear ambitions. North Korea's pursuit of nuclear weapons has led to international sanctions and diplomatic efforts aimed at denuclearization, but the regime's strategic calculus remains centered on maintaining its nuclear deterrent. The United States, South Korea, and Japan have all engaged in various diplomatic efforts to address the North Korean threat, while China, as North Korea's primary ally and economic partner, is important in influencing the regime's behavior. The ongoing security concerns on the Korean Peninsula underscore the broader geopolitical competition in Northeast Asia.

Southeast Asia, with its strategic location and diverse political landscape, is another important area in Asian geopolitics. The Association of Southeast Asian Nations (ASEAN) plays a central role in regional diplomacy, promoting economic integration and conflict resolution. However, ASEAN's unity is often tested by the differing interests of its member states, particularly in relation to China. While some ASEAN countries have deep economic ties with China, others are wary of its growing influence and assertiveness, particularly in the South China Sea. The balancing act between engaging China economically while hedging against its strategic ambitions is a common theme in the region's foreign policies.

Africa's Role in Global Affairs

Africa's role in global affairs has evolved significantly over the past few decades, shaped by its vast natural resources, strategic location, and growing economic potential. **While historically marginalized in international relations, Africa is increasingly recognized as a key player in global geopolitics, economics, and diplomacy.** The continent's diverse and dynamic nature makes it a crucial area of focus for major powers and international organizations.

One of the most significant aspects of Africa's role in global affairs is its abundance of natural resources. The continent is rich in minerals, oil, gas, and agricultural products, making it a vital supplier of raw materials to the global economy. Countries like Nigeria, Angola, and Libya are major oil producers, while the Democratic Republic of the Congo is a leading source of cobalt, essential for modern technology. The competition for access to Africa's resources has driven foreign investment and diplomatic engagement from countries like China, the United States, and the European Union. China, in particular, has established a strong presence in Africa through its Belt and Road Initiative (BRI), investing in infrastructure projects across the continent in exchange for access to resources and markets.

Africa's strategic location, particularly along key maritime routes, also contributes to its importance in global affairs. The Horn of Africa, for example, sits near the Bab-el-Mandeb Strait, a critical chokepoint for global shipping. The region's proximity to the Middle East and Europe makes it a strategic area for military and economic interests, leading to a significant international naval presence in the Gulf of Aden and the Red Sea. Djibouti, located at the crossroads of these vital maritime routes, hosts military bases from several countries, including the United States, China, and France, reflecting the strategic importance of the region.

The African Union (AU) plays a central role in representing Africa's interests on the global stage. Established in 2002, the AU aims to promote political and economic integration, peace, and stability across the continent. The organization has been instrumental in mediating conflicts, supporting democratic transitions, and addressing issues such as climate change and public health. The AU's increasing involvement in global diplomacy is evident in its participation in international forums like the United Nations, where it advocates for the continent's interests, including calls for reforms to the UN Security Council to reflect Africa's growing influence.

Africa's economic potential is another factor that enhances its role in global affairs. The continent is home to some of the world's fastest-growing economies, driven by a young and expanding population, urbanization, and technological adoption. The African Continental Free Trade Area (AfCFTA), launched in 2021, is one of the most ambitious efforts to boost intra-African trade and economic integration. By creating a single market of over 1.2 billion people, the AfCFTA has the potential to transform Africa's economic landscape, making it a more significant player in global trade and investment. Foreign investors are increasingly looking to Africa for opportunities in sectors such as telecommunications, fintech, and renewable energy, recognizing the continent's potential for growth and innovation.

Africa's role in global security is also notable, particularly in the context of counterterrorism and peacekeeping. The continent has been a focal point in the global fight against terrorism, with extremist groups like Boko Haram, al-Shabaab, and ISIS-affiliated factions operating in various regions. The United States, France, and other international partners have provided military support to African countries to combat these threats, while the AU and regional organizations have also played active roles in peacekeeping and counterterrorism efforts. The continent's peacekeeping missions, often in partnership with the United Nations, are critical to maintaining stability in conflict-prone areas such as the Sahel, Central Africa, and the Horn of Africa.

Climate change is another critical issue where Africa has a key role in global affairs. The continent is highly vulnerable to the impacts of climate change, including droughts, desertification, and rising sea levels. African nations have been active participants in international climate negotiations, advocating for greater support for adaptation and mitigation efforts. The continent's vast potential for renewable energy, particularly solar and wind power, positions it as a key player in the global transition to sustainable energy sources. However, Africa's ability to address climate change is constrained by limited financial and technical resources, highlighting the need for increased international cooperation and support.

Africa's diplomatic engagement with major global powers is multifaceted and reflects the continent's diverse interests and priorities. China has emerged as Africa's largest trading partner and a significant source of investment, while the United States has focused on security cooperation and development assistance through initiatives like the African Growth and Opportunity Act (AGOA). **The European Union remains a key partner for Africa, particularly in areas such as trade, development aid, and migration management.** However, African countries are increasingly asserting their agency in international relations, seeking to diversify their partnerships and avoid over-reliance on any single power.

Latin American Politics and International Relations

Latin America is a region of diverse political landscapes, economic challenges, and strategic importance in global affairs. **The region's history of colonization, dictatorship, and economic dependency has shaped its contemporary political dynamics and its role in international relations.** Today, Latin America is characterized by a mix of democratic and authoritarian regimes, varying levels of economic development, and complex relationships with global powers.

The United States has historically been the most influential external actor in Latin American politics and international relations. The Monroe Doctrine, articulated in 1823, established the Western Hemisphere as a sphere of U.S. influence, leading to a long history of intervention in Latin American affairs. During the Cold War, the U.S. supported anti-communist regimes and movements across the region, often through covert operations and military interventions, as seen in countries like Chile, Nicaragua, and Guatemala. The legacy of these interventions continues to shape U.S.-Latin American relations, with issues like migration, drug trafficking, and trade dominating the agenda.

In recent years, however, Latin America has sought to diversify its international partnerships, engaging more actively with other global powers. China has emerged as a major economic partner for many Latin American countries, investing heavily in infrastructure, mining, and agriculture. **China's trade with Latin America has grown exponentially, making it the region's second-largest trading partner after the United States.** This growing economic relationship has led to closer political ties, with Latin American countries increasingly looking to China as an alternative to U.S. influence. **However, this shift has also raised concerns about economic dependency on China and the potential for exploitation of the region's natural resources.**

Brazil, the largest and most populous country in Latin America, has an important part in regional and global politics. As a member of the BRICS group (Brazil, Russia, India, China, and South Africa), Brazil has sought to position itself as a leader of the Global South, advocating for greater representation of developing countries in international institutions. Brazil's foreign policy has traditionally focused on regional integration, particularly through organizations like Mercosur and the Union of South American Nations (UNASUR). However, domestic political and economic challenges, including corruption scandals and economic recession, have limited Brazil's ability to fully realize its potential as a global power.

Venezuela's political and economic crisis is another major issue in Latin American politics with significant international implications. The country, once one of the wealthiest in the region due to its vast oil reserves, has been plunged into a severe crisis under the leadership of Nicolás Maduro. Widespread corruption, economic mismanagement, and political repression have led to hyperinflation, food shortages, and mass migration, with millions of Venezuelans fleeing to neighboring countries. The international community is deeply divided on how to address the crisis, with the United States and several Latin American countries recognizing opposition leader Juan Guaidó as Venezuela's legitimate president, while Russia, China, and others continue to support Maduro. The crisis in Venezuela has highlighted the broader struggle for influence in Latin America, with global powers competing to shape the region's political future.

Regional integration has long been a goal in Latin American politics, though it has faced numerous challenges. Organizations like the Organization of American States (OAS), Mercosur, and the Pacific Alliance have sought to promote economic cooperation and political dialogue in the region. However, ideological differences, economic disparities, and external pressures have often hindered these efforts. The rise of leftist governments in the early 2000s, known as the "Pink Tide," led to a wave of regional solidarity and anti-U.S. sentiment, with countries like Venezuela, Bolivia, and Ecuador pushing for greater independence from

Washington. However, the subsequent economic downturn and political shifts in countries like Brazil and Argentina have led to a more mixed political landscape, with some countries embracing market-oriented policies while others maintain a more populist approach.

Latin America's relationship with Europe, particularly through the European Union, is also significant. The EU has sought to strengthen its ties with the region through trade agreements, development aid, and political dialogue. The EU-Mercosur trade agreement, negotiated over two decades, is one of the most significant efforts to deepen economic ties between the two regions. However, concerns over environmental issues, particularly deforestation in the Amazon, have led to delays in ratifying the agreement, reflecting the growing importance of sustainability in international relations.

Migration is another key issue in Latin American politics and international relations. The region has been a source of significant migration flows, particularly to the United States, driven by factors such as economic instability, violence, and political repression. The migration crisis at the U.S.-Mexico border has become a central issue in U.S.-Latin American relations, with significant implications for domestic politics in both the United States and Latin American countries. The issue of migration also highlights broader challenges of inequality and governance in the region, as well as the need for comprehensive international cooperation to address its root causes.

CHAPTER 12: THE ROLE OF TECHNOLOGY IN INTERNATIONAL RELATIONS

Cybersecurity and Global Politics

Cybersecurity has become a central issue in global politics, reflecting the increasing reliance of nations on digital infrastructure and the internet. **As countries, businesses, and individuals become more interconnected, the potential for cyberattacks to disrupt critical systems and steal sensitive information has grown significantly.** This has led to cybersecurity being recognized not only as a technical challenge but also as a critical aspect of national security and international relations.

Nation-states are both key players and major targets in the realm of cybersecurity. Governments rely on digital networks for everything from military operations and intelligence gathering to critical infrastructure like energy grids and financial systems. This reliance makes them vulnerable to cyberattacks, which can be launched by other states, criminal organizations, or even independent hackers. The complexity of the cyber landscape, where attacks can be difficult to trace and attribute, adds to the challenge of defending against these threats.

State-sponsored cyberattacks have become a tool of modern warfare and espionage, blurring the lines between peace and conflict. Countries like Russia, China, Iran, and North Korea have been accused of conducting cyberattacks against other states, targeting government agencies, businesses, and infrastructure. These attacks can range from stealing classified information and intellectual property to disrupting critical systems. For example, the 2017 WannaCry ransomware attack, attributed to North Korea, affected hundreds of thousands of computers worldwide, including systems in hospitals and businesses. Similarly, the SolarWinds hack in 2020, believed to be orchestrated by Russia, infiltrated numerous U.S. government agencies and private companies, exposing sensitive data and highlighting the vulnerability of even the most secure networks.

Cybersecurity is not only about defense; it is also a tool for power projection and influence. States use cyber capabilities to achieve strategic objectives, such as undermining an adversary's economic stability, influencing political processes, or gaining a technological edge. For instance, during the 2016 U.S. presidential election, Russian actors conducted a cyber campaign to influence the outcome, using hacking and disinformation to sow discord and weaken public trust in democratic institutions. This incident underscores how cyber operations can have far-reaching consequences, extending beyond immediate technical damage to influence broader geopolitical dynamics.

International law and norms around cybersecurity are still evolving, reflecting the challenges of regulating actions in cyberspace. Unlike conventional warfare, where clear rules exist under international law, the rules governing state behavior in cyberspace are less defined. This ambiguity allows states to exploit the grey areas of cyber operations, often engaging in activities that fall short of an armed attack but still cause significant harm. Efforts to establish international norms and agreements on cybersecurity, such as those promoted by the United Nations, face significant hurdles due to differing national interests and the difficulty of enforcing compliance in the digital domain.

The private sector plays a critical role in global cybersecurity, as much of the world's digital infrastructure is owned and operated by private companies. Tech giants like Microsoft, Google, and Amazon have vast amounts of data and are integral to the functioning of the global internet. These companies are often on the front lines of defending against cyberattacks and have a key role in setting security standards and responding to breaches. However, the relationship between the private sector and governments can be complex, with issues around data privacy, surveillance, and the extent of cooperation in national security matters often causing tension.

International cooperation on cybersecurity is essential but challenging. Cyber threats do not respect national borders, making it crucial for countries to work together to share information, develop joint responses, and build resilience. Organizations like NATO have recognized cybersecurity as a key area of focus, with member states agreeing to mutual defense in the event of a significant cyberattack. However, trust issues and geopolitical rivalries can hinder cooperation, especially when states suspect each other of engaging in cyber espionage or attacks.

Cybersecurity's role in global politics will continue to grow as technology advances and the world becomes more interconnected. The challenge lies in balancing the benefits of the digital age with the risks it poses, ensuring that the global community can navigate this complex landscape while safeguarding security and stability.

The Impact of Social Media on Diplomacy

Social media has transformed the way diplomacy is conducted, providing both new opportunities and challenges for international relations. **The rise of platforms like Twitter, Facebook, and Instagram has enabled diplomats, governments, and international organizations to communicate directly with global audiences in real-time.** This direct communication has altered traditional diplomatic practices, making diplomacy more immediate, transparent, and, in some cases, unpredictable.

One of the most significant impacts of social media on diplomacy is the ability to reach and engage with the public on a global scale. In the past, diplomatic communication was primarily conducted through formal channels, such as press releases, official statements, and private negotiations. Today, social media allows diplomats to bypass these traditional methods and speak directly to both domestic and international audiences. This has democratized access to diplomatic information, allowing people from around the world to follow and respond to diplomatic developments as they happen.

Social media has also become a tool for public diplomacy, where countries use these platforms to promote their image, values, and policies to the world. For example, governments and embassies regularly use social media to highlight cultural events, share national achievements, and respond to global issues. This kind of engagement helps build soft power, enhancing a country's influence by shaping perceptions and fostering goodwill among foreign publics. The U.S. State Department's use of Twitter to engage with global audiences, particularly during crises, is a notable example of how social media is used in public diplomacy.

However, the immediacy and accessibility of social media also present challenges for diplomacy. The speed at which information spreads on social media can lead to hasty or ill-considered statements that may have diplomatic repercussions. **Diplomatic gaffes, misunderstandings, or even deliberately provocative statements made on social media can escalate tensions between countries.** Additionally, the spread of misinformation and propaganda on social media platforms can complicate diplomatic efforts by creating confusion and undermining trust.

Social media has also introduced a new level of transparency in diplomatic affairs. While this can increase accountability and public engagement, it can also limit the discretion traditionally afforded to diplomats. Sensitive negotiations or diplomatic efforts that require confidentiality can be jeopardized by leaks or unauthorized social media posts. As a result, diplomats must navigate the fine line between maintaining transparency and protecting sensitive information.

The use of social media by world leaders has further complicated traditional diplomatic protocols. Leaders like Donald Trump, who famously used Twitter as a primary communication tool during his presidency, have demonstrated how social media can be used to bypass traditional diplomatic channels. This direct and often unfiltered communication can disrupt established diplomatic practices, sometimes leading to diplomatic tensions or crises. At the same time, it has also allowed leaders to shape global narratives and respond quickly to international events, demonstrating the dual-edged nature of social media in diplomacy.

In summary, social media has fundamentally changed the landscape of diplomacy, offering new ways for engagement and communication while also introducing challenges that diplomats must carefully manage. As social media continues to evolve, its role in shaping international relations will likely grow, requiring diplomats and governments to adapt their strategies to navigate this dynamic and often unpredictable environment.

Technological Warfare and Defense Systems

Technological advancements have revolutionized warfare and defense systems, fundamentally altering the nature of military conflict and international security. **From precision-guided munitions and unmanned aerial vehicles (UAVs) to cyber warfare and artificial intelligence (AI), technology has become a critical factor in modern warfare, shaping the strategies and capabilities of nations.**

One of the most significant developments in technological warfare is the rise of precision-guided munitions (PGMs). These weapons, equipped with advanced targeting systems, allow for highly accurate strikes on enemy targets, minimizing collateral damage and increasing the effectiveness of military operations. PGMs have been used extensively in conflicts such as the Gulf War, the Iraq War, and the ongoing conflict in Syria, demonstrating their capability to change the dynamics of the battlefield. The use of these weapons allows military forces to achieve objectives with greater precision and efficiency, reducing the need for large-scale troop deployments.

Unmanned systems, particularly drones, have also become a central component of modern military strategies. UAVs, both armed and unarmed, are used for a variety of purposes, including surveillance, reconnaissance, and targeted strikes. Drones offer significant advantages in terms of operational flexibility and risk reduction, as they can be deployed in dangerous environments without putting human lives at risk. The use of drones for targeted killings, such as the U.S. drone strike that killed Iranian General Qasem Soleimani in 2020, highlights the growing role of these systems in strategic military operations. However, the use of drones has also raised ethical and legal concerns, particularly regarding the implications for sovereignty and the potential for civilian casualties.

Cyber warfare represents another critical aspect of technological advancements in defense systems. As military and civilian infrastructure become increasingly digitized, the potential for cyberattacks to disrupt critical systems and cause significant damage has grown. Cyber warfare can target a wide range of systems, including communication networks, power grids, financial systems, and even military command and control centers. The 2007 cyberattacks on Estonia, widely attributed to Russian actors, demonstrated the potential for cyber warfare to paralyze a nation's infrastructure without the need for traditional military force. Cyber operations are now a key component of military strategy, with countries investing heavily in both offensive and defensive cyber capabilities.

Artificial intelligence (AI) is another area of technological advancement that is poised to reshape warfare and defense systems. AI has the potential to enhance decision-making, improve the accuracy of weapons systems, and enable autonomous operations. For example, AI can be used to analyze vast amounts of data to identify potential threats or optimize the deployment of military resources. Additionally, AI-driven systems can operate in environments that are too dangerous or complex for human soldiers, such as unmanned submarines or autonomous aircraft. However, the integration of AI into military systems also raises significant ethical and strategic questions, particularly regarding the potential for autonomous weapons to make life-and-death decisions without human oversight.

Space has become an increasingly contested domain in technological warfare. The militarization of space, with the development of anti-satellite weapons and the deployment of military satellites, reflects the growing importance of space assets for military operations. **Satellites are crucial for communication, navigation, intelligence, and missile detection, making them a strategic target in any conflict.** The development of space-based weapons and the potential for conflict in space pose new challenges for international security, requiring the development of norms and agreements to prevent an arms race in this domain.

The proliferation of these advanced technologies has also led to changes in defense strategies and military doctrines. Nations are increasingly focusing on developing multi-domain operations, integrating capabilities across land, sea, air, cyber, and space to achieve strategic objectives. This approach reflects the recognition that modern conflicts are likely to be fought across multiple domains simultaneously, requiring coordinated and integrated responses. The concept of multi-domain operations highlights the complexity of modern warfare and the need for adaptable and resilient defense systems.

However, the rapid pace of technological advancements also presents challenges for global security. The development and deployment of new technologies can lead to arms races, as nations seek to maintain or gain a technological edge over their rivals. This dynamic is evident in the ongoing competition between the United States, China, and Russia in areas such as AI, cyber capabilities, and hypersonic weapons. Additionally, the diffusion of these technologies to non-state actors, such as terrorist organizations or rogue states, increases the potential for asymmetric warfare, where technologically advanced weapons are used against conventional forces or civilian targets.

Global Communication Networks and Diplomacy

Global communication networks have become a fundamental aspect of modern diplomacy, transforming how countries interact, negotiate, and influence one another. **These networks, comprising the internet, satellite communications,** and various digital platforms, allow for the rapid exchange of information across the globe, breaking down barriers and enabling real-time diplomacy. The impact of these networks on international relations is profound, as they not only facilitate official diplomatic communications but also influence public opinion, shape global narratives, and support soft power strategies.

One of the most significant effects of global communication networks on diplomacy is the speed at which information can be shared and decisions can be made. In the past, diplomatic communication was often slow, relying on messengers, letters, or telegrams to convey messages between capitals. Today, diplomats can communicate instantly with their counterparts and their home governments through secure digital channels. This immediacy allows for more responsive and flexible diplomacy, particularly in crisis situations where rapid decision-making is crucial.

Global communication networks have also democratized access to information and diplomatic engagement. In the digital age, governments, international organizations, and non-state actors can communicate directly with global audiences, bypassing traditional media and diplomatic channels. Social media platforms, in particular, have become powerful tools for public diplomacy, where states can promote their policies, engage with foreign publics, and respond to global events in real-time. This has shifted the landscape of diplomacy, making it more public and transparent, but also more prone to the challenges of misinformation and propaganda.

Another important aspect of global communication networks in diplomacy is their role in shaping global narratives and public opinion. The internet and social media enable the rapid spread of information, but they also allow for the dissemination of disinformation and influence campaigns. Countries use these networks to project their narratives, shape perceptions, and influence political outcomes in other states. For example, during elections or political crises, global communication networks can be used to sway public opinion or undermine the credibility of opponents, often leading to diplomatic tensions or conflicts.

The integration of global communication networks into diplomatic practice has also led to the rise of digital diplomacy, or "e-diplomacy." This involves the use of digital tools and platforms to conduct diplomacy, engage with foreign publics, and manage international relations. **E-diplomacy includes activities such as online negotiations, virtual summits, and the use of data analytics to inform diplomatic strategies.** As more countries embrace digital diplomacy, it is becoming an essential component of modern international relations, allowing states to adapt to the digital age while maintaining their diplomatic influence.

However, the reliance on global communication networks also presents challenges for diplomacy. The risk of cyberattacks on diplomatic communications, the spread of false information, and the potential for digital surveillance by foreign powers are all significant concerns. Ensuring the security and integrity of diplomatic communications in this digital environment is critical, as breaches can lead to diplomatic incidents or undermine trust between states. Moreover, the rapid pace of information flow can sometimes lead to hasty decisions or miscommunications, making it essential for diplomats to balance speed with accuracy and caution.

Space Exploration and International Cooperation

Space exploration has long been a symbol of technological achievement and national pride, but it has also become a platform for international cooperation. **As humanity ventures further into space, collaboration among countries has become increasingly important, both for sharing the costs and risks of space missions and for advancing scientific knowledge.** The complexities of space exploration, combined with the vast resources required, have made international cooperation a practical necessity and a diplomatic opportunity.

One of the most prominent examples of international cooperation in space exploration is the International Space Station (ISS). The ISS is a joint project involving the United States, Russia, Canada, Japan, and the European Space Agency (ESA). Launched in 1998, the ISS serves as a model of how countries with diverse political interests can work together towards common scientific goals. Astronauts from different nations live and work together on the ISS, conducting research that benefits humanity as a whole, from studying the effects of microgravity on the human body to advancing our understanding of materials science.

Space exploration has also led to numerous bilateral and multilateral agreements aimed at ensuring the peaceful use of outer space. The Outer Space Treaty of 1967, signed by over 100 countries, is the cornerstone of international space law, establishing that space exploration should be conducted for the benefit of all humankind and that space should be free from military use, except for peaceful purposes. This treaty reflects a shared understanding that space should remain a global commons, not dominated by any one nation, and that international cooperation is essential for maintaining this principle.

In addition to these formal agreements, space exploration has fostered informal cooperation and partnerships among countries. For example, space agencies often share data and resources for satellite missions, planetary exploration, and space observation. NASA's collaboration with the Indian Space Research Organisation (ISRO) on the Mars Orbiter Mission is one such example, where data sharing and joint analysis have enhanced the scientific output of both missions. These partnerships not only advance scientific knowledge but also strengthen diplomatic ties and build trust between nations.

The growing involvement of private companies in space exploration has also opened new avenues for international cooperation. Companies like SpaceX, Blue Origin, and others are not only advancing space technology but are also facilitating collaboration between nations and the private sector. For instance, SpaceX's role in launching astronauts to the ISS under NASA's Commercial Crew Program has demonstrated how public-private partnerships can complement international cooperation efforts. As more countries and companies enter the space race, the potential for new forms of collaboration, as well as competition, is likely to increase.

However, space exploration is not without its geopolitical challenges. The dual-use nature of space technology, which can be used for both civilian and military purposes, raises concerns about the militarization of space. The development of anti-satellite weapons and the strategic importance of space-based assets, such as communication and navigation satellites, have led to increasing tensions among major powers. Countries like the United States, China, and Russia are investing heavily in space defense capabilities, reflecting the growing recognition that space is not just a domain for exploration, but also a potential battleground.

Moreover, as more countries develop their space programs, there is a need for updated international frameworks to manage space traffic, debris, and resource utilization. The potential for conflicts over space resources, such as the mining of asteroids or the moon, is becoming a significant concern. **Efforts to establish new international agreements or update existing ones, like the Artemis Accords initiated by NASA, aim to ensure that space exploration remains peaceful and cooperative, even as competition intensifies.**

So while space exploration has brought countries together to achieve remarkable scientific and technological advancements, it also requires careful management of geopolitical tensions and the development of new norms to ensure that space remains a domain of peaceful exploration for all humanity.

CHAPTER 13: INTERNATIONAL RELATIONS IN THE POST-COLD WAR ERA

The End of the Cold War and its Global Impact

The end of the Cold War marked a profound shift in global politics, redefining international relations and altering the balance of power across the world. **The collapse of the Soviet Union in 1991 effectively ended the ideological struggle between capitalism and communism that had dominated global affairs for nearly half a century.** This period saw the dissolution of the bipolar world order, where the United States and the Soviet Union had been the two superpowers, each leading their respective blocs.

One of the most immediate impacts of the Cold War's end was the unification of Germany. The fall of the Berlin Wall in 1989 symbolized the collapse of communist regimes in Eastern Europe. Germany, divided since the end of World War II, was reunified in 1990, becoming a powerful symbol of the end of division in Europe. This unification not only marked the physical and ideological reunification of a country but also signaled a broader realignment in Europe, where former communist states sought integration with the West.

The dissolution of the Soviet Union itself had far-reaching consequences. Fifteen new independent states emerged from the former Soviet Union, with Russia inheriting the Soviet Union's seat on the United Nations Security Council and its nuclear arsenal. These new nations, such as Ukraine, Belarus, and the Baltic states, had to navigate the transition from communism to democracy and market economies, often facing significant political and economic challenges. The emergence of these states also introduced new dynamics in regional and global politics, as they sought to establish their identities and place in the international community.

The end of the Cold War also led to the expansion of NATO and the European Union. With the collapse of the Warsaw Pact, many Eastern European countries, once under Soviet influence, sought closer ties with the West. NATO expanded its membership to include former communist states, such as Poland, Hungary, and the Czech Republic, in the 1990s, a move that Russia viewed with increasing suspicion. Similarly, the European Union expanded eastward, incorporating countries that had once been behind the Iron Curtain. This expansion helped stabilize these countries economically and politically but also created new tensions with Russia, which saw the encroachment of Western institutions as a threat to its sphere of influence.

The end of the Cold War also marked the beginning of the United States' unipolar moment. With the Soviet Union gone, the U.S. emerged as the world's sole superpower, exerting significant influence over global affairs. **This period saw the U.S. leading efforts to promote democracy, liberalize trade, and intervene in conflicts around the world, often under the banner of humanitarian intervention.** The Gulf War in 1991, where a U.S.-led coalition expelled Iraqi forces from Kuwait, was one of the first major conflicts in the post-Cold War era, demonstrating the U.S.'s military dominance and willingness to act as the global policeman.

However, the unipolar moment also brought challenges and new conflicts. The absence of a rival superpower did not lead to global peace; instead, new conflicts emerged, particularly in regions where Cold War dynamics had suppressed underlying tensions. The breakup of Yugoslavia in the 1990s led to a series of brutal ethnic conflicts, including the Bosnian War, which saw widespread atrocities and the first genocide in Europe since World War II. The international community's response to these conflicts, particularly NATO's intervention in Kosovo in 1999, highlighted the new challenges of humanitarian intervention and the difficulties of building a new world order based on liberal values.

Economically, the end of the Cold War accelerated globalization. With the ideological barrier of communism removed, markets opened up, and trade expanded across borders at an unprecedented rate. Former communist countries transitioned to market economies, and China, while maintaining its political system, embraced economic reforms that would eventually turn it into a global economic powerhouse. This shift contributed to the rapid growth of global trade and investment, but it also led to new economic challenges, such as the rise of economic inequality and the vulnerabilities exposed by global financial crises.

The end of the Cold War also reshaped global institutions. The United Nations, freed from the paralysis often caused by U.S.-Soviet rivalry, took on a more active role in peacekeeping and conflict resolution. However, the challenges of the post-Cold War world also exposed the limitations of these institutions, as seen in their struggles to address conflicts in Somalia, Rwanda, and the Balkans. The need for reform in global governance became apparent, but efforts to adapt these institutions to the new realities of a multipolar world have often been slow and contentious.

In the post-Cold War era, international relations have become more complex and multipolar. New powers, such as China and India, have risen, challenging the dominance of the West and creating a more distributed balance of power. Global issues like terrorism, climate change, and cyber threats have also emerged as critical challenges, requiring new forms of international cooperation. The end of the Cold War was not just the conclusion of a bipolar rivalry; it was the beginning of a new, more interconnected, and interdependent world, with its own set of opportunities and challenges.

Unipolarity vs. Multipolarity

In international relations, the terms unipolarity and multipolarity describe the distribution of power in the global system. **Unipolarity refers to a world dominated by a single superpower, while multipolarity involves multiple powerful states or blocs that share influence.** The transition from a unipolar to a multipolar world, or the coexistence of these two dynamics, has profound implications for global stability, diplomacy, and conflict.

The post-Cold War era is often characterized by unipolarity, with the United States emerging as the dominant global power after the collapse of the Soviet Union. During this period, the U.S. enjoyed unparalleled military, economic, and cultural influence, shaping global norms and institutions. This unipolar moment allowed the U.S. to promote its vision of a liberal international order, characterized by open markets, democratic governance, and multilateral institutions. American power was evident in its ability to lead international coalitions, as seen in the Gulf War and interventions in the Balkans, and in its dominance in global economic institutions like the World Bank and the International Monetary Fund (IMF).

However, unipolarity also faced criticism and resistance. Some argued that the concentration of power in one state led to unilateralism, where the U.S. acted without sufficient regard for the views or interests of other countries. The 2003 invasion of Iraq, led by the U.S. without broad international support, exemplified this concern and fueled global debate about the legitimacy and consequences of unipolarity. Moreover, the costs of maintaining a unipolar world, both in terms of military expenditures and global responsibilities, raised questions about the sustainability of this system.

Multipolarity, by contrast, describes a world where multiple states hold significant power, creating a more balanced distribution of influence. This system is often seen as more stable because power is not concentrated in one state, reducing the likelihood of unilateral actions and fostering cooperation among great powers. In a multipolar world, power dynamics are more fluid, with shifting alliances and balances of power that require constant negotiation and diplomacy. The European balance of power in the 19th century is often cited as a historical example of a multipolar system, where no single state dominated, and stability was maintained through a complex web of alliances.

The rise of other powers, particularly China and Russia, has challenged the unipolarity of the post-Cold War era, leading to discussions about a return to multipolarity. China's rapid economic growth and increasing military capabilities have positioned it as a potential rival to the U.S., while Russia, despite its smaller economy, continues to exert influence through its military strength and energy resources. These developments suggest a shift towards a more multipolar world, where multiple states, including the European Union, India, and regional powers, have significant roles in shaping global outcomes.

Multipolarity can foster greater cooperation as states work together to address global challenges. For example, climate change, global health, and terrorism are issues that require collective action, and a multipolar world might encourage more inclusive and multilateral approaches. **However, multipolarity also carries risks, particularly if it leads to increased competition and conflict among great powers.** The lack of a clear hegemon can create uncertainty, and rivalries between emerging powers can lead to instability, as seen in the build-up to World War I.

One of the key debates in international relations is whether multipolarity or unipolarity offers greater global stability. Proponents of unipolarity argue that a dominant power can enforce rules and provide public goods, such as security and economic stability, reducing the likelihood of conflict. In contrast, supporters of multipolarity contend that a more distributed power structure reduces the chances of one state imposing its will on others, leading to a more balanced and just international order. The answer may depend on how power is exercised and whether it is perceived as legitimate by other states.

The Rise of China and Emerging Powers

The rise of China and other emerging powers has been one of the most significant developments in international relations in the 21st century. **China's rapid economic growth, military modernization, and expanding global influence have positioned it as a key challenger to the United States' dominance, leading to shifts in the global balance of power.** Alongside China, other emerging powers, such as India, Brazil, and Russia, are also reshaping the international system, challenging established norms and creating a more multipolar world.

China's economic transformation is at the heart of its rise. Since the late 1970s, China has implemented market-oriented reforms that have propelled it from a relatively poor, agrarian society to the world's second-largest economy. China's integration into the global economy, particularly after joining the World Trade Organization (WTO) in 2001, has enabled it to become a major player in global trade and investment. Chinese companies are now among the largest in the world, and the country is a leading exporter of goods, from electronics to textiles. This economic power has translated into greater political and diplomatic influence, as China leverages its economic relationships to build strategic partnerships and extend its influence in regions like Africa, Latin America, and Southeast Asia.

China's Belt and Road Initiative (BRI) is a key example of how it is using economic power to expand its global influence. Launched in 2013, the BRI is an ambitious infrastructure and investment project that aims to connect Asia, Europe, and Africa through a network of railways, ports, and highways. **The initiative has attracted participation from over 60 countries and has the potential to reshape global trade routes and economic relationships.** However, the BRI has also raised concerns about debt dependency and China's strategic intentions, with critics arguing that it could lead to a form of economic imperialism.

Militarily, China has also been rapidly modernizing its armed forces, with a particular focus on its navy, air force, and missile capabilities. The People's Liberation Army (PLA) is now one of the world's largest and most technologically advanced military forces. China's assertiveness in the South China Sea, where it has built artificial islands and established military bases, has heightened tensions with its neighbors and the United States. This militarization, combined with China's growing economic power, has led to concerns about a new form of great power competition reminiscent of the Cold War.

China's rise is often seen in the context of broader shifts in global power, with other emerging economies also playing increasingly important roles. India, with its large population and rapidly growing economy, is another key player in this emerging multipolar world. India's economic growth, driven by a burgeoning technology sector and a growing middle class, has made it a significant market and a rising power in its own right. India's strategic location and its role in regional organizations, such as the South Asian Association for Regional Cooperation (SAARC), further enhance its influence in Asia.

Brazil and Russia are also important emerging powers, each with its own unique strengths and challenges. Brazil, as the largest economy in Latin America, is important in regional and global trade, particularly in commodities like agriculture and minerals. However, Brazil has faced significant political and economic challenges in recent years, which have limited its ability to fully capitalize on its potential as a global power. Russia, despite its economic challenges and demographic decline, remains a significant military power with a permanent seat on the United Nations Security Council. Russia's assertiveness in its near abroad, particularly in Ukraine and Syria, demonstrates its willingness to use military force to protect its interests and challenge Western influence.

The rise of these emerging powers is contributing to a shift towards a more multipolar world, where no single country dominates the international system. This shift presents both opportunities and challenges for global governance. On one hand, the inclusion of more voices in international decision-making could lead to more balanced and representative global institutions. On the other hand, the competition between emerging powers and established powers could lead to greater instability, as countries jostle for influence and pursue conflicting interests.

The rise of China and other emerging powers also raises questions about the future of the liberal international order. These countries, particularly China and Russia, often challenge the norms and institutions that have governed the international system since the end of World War II. Whether this will lead to a fundamental transformation of the global order, or whether these emerging powers will be integrated into existing institutions, remains an open question.

The Role of the United States in the New World Order

The United States has played a central role in shaping the global order since the end of World War II, and this role has evolved significantly in the post-Cold War era. **As the world's leading military and economic power, the U.S. has been instrumental in establishing and maintaining the international system that governs global politics, economics, and security.** However, the rise of new powers, shifting global dynamics, and domestic challenges have led to questions about the future role of the U.S. in the new world order.

In the immediate aftermath of the Cold War, the United States emerged as the world's sole superpower, enjoying what many referred to as a "unipolar moment." This period was characterized by U.S. dominance in global affairs, with the country playing a leading role in promoting democracy, free markets, and multilateral institutions. The U.S. led efforts to expand NATO, intervene in conflicts in the Balkans and the Middle East, and shape the global economy through institutions like the World Trade Organization (WTO) and the International Monetary Fund (IMF). This unipolarity allowed the U.S. to influence global norms and policies in ways that reflected its values and interests.

However, the post-Cold War unipolarity also brought challenges and criticisms. The U.S.'s role as a global policeman was increasingly questioned, particularly in the wake of the 2003 invasion of Iraq, which was widely criticized for its unilateralism and its consequences for regional stability. The financial crisis of 2008 further exposed vulnerabilities in the U.S.-led global economic system, leading to a decline in American soft power and raising doubts about the sustainability of U.S. hegemony. These developments have contributed to a gradual shift towards a more multipolar world, where other countries, particularly China, are beginning to challenge U.S. dominance.

Despite these challenges, the United States continues to be important in the new world order, particularly in terms of global security and economic leadership. The U.S. maintains the world's most powerful military, with a global network of alliances and bases that allow it to project power across the globe. This military presence is a key component of the U.S.'s ability to deter potential adversaries and respond to global crises. The U.S. also remains a central player in global economic governance, with its influence in institutions like the IMF, World Bank, and G7 continuing to shape global economic policies.

The U.S. role in the new world order is also defined by its relationships with other major powers, particularly China and Russia. The U.S.-China relationship is arguably the most important bilateral relationship in the world today, with significant implications for global trade, security, and climate change. While the two countries are economic competitors, their interdependence means that cooperation is necessary on issues like trade, technology, and climate action. At the same time, the U.S.-Russia relationship is characterized by strategic competition, particularly in areas like cyber security, nuclear arms control, and influence in Eastern Europe. The U.S.'s ability to manage these complex relationships will be crucial in shaping the future of global stability.

The United States also plays a key role in promoting and defending the liberal international order, which is based on principles such as democracy, human rights, and the rule of law. This role has been challenged in recent years, both by the rise of authoritarian powers like China and Russia and by domestic challenges within the U.S. itself. The Trump administration's "America First" policy, which saw a retreat from multilateralism and a focus on national sovereignty, raised concerns about the U.S.'s commitment to the international order it helped create. However, the Biden administration has sought to restore U.S. leadership in global governance, rejoining international agreements like the Paris Climate Accord and reaffirming alliances with democratic countries.

Looking forward, the role of the United States in the new world order will likely involve a combination of leadership, cooperation, and adaptation to a changing global landscape. The U.S. will need to work with emerging powers, manage great power competition, and address global challenges like climate change, pandemics, and technological change. At the same time, the U.S. must also address its domestic challenges, including political polarization and economic inequality, which have implications for its ability to lead on the global stage.

CHAPTER 14: GLOBAL HEALTH AND INTERNATIONAL RELATIONS

The Impact of Global Pandemics

Global pandemics have a profound impact on international relations, reshaping how nations interact, cooperate, and respond to crises. **These health emergencies transcend borders, affecting not just public health but also economies, security, and diplomacy.** The COVID-19 pandemic, for instance, highlighted the interconnectedness of the world and underscored the importance of global cooperation in managing health crises.

One of the immediate impacts of global pandemics is the strain on international health systems and economies. When a pandemic strikes, countries are forced to divert resources to manage the outbreak, often at the expense of other critical areas. This can lead to economic downturns, as seen with COVID-19, where global supply chains were disrupted, businesses closed, and unemployment soared. The economic fallout from pandemics often leads to increased tensions between countries, especially when it comes to the distribution of scarce resources like vaccines and medical supplies.

Global pandemics also affect diplomatic relations. During a pandemic, the need for international cooperation becomes paramount, but it can also strain relationships. Countries may compete for limited medical supplies, as seen during the early stages of the COVID-19 pandemic, when nations scrambled for personal protective equipment (PPE) and ventilators. This competition can lead to accusations of "vaccine nationalism," where wealthier nations prioritize their own populations over global distribution, creating friction between countries.

The role of international organizations becomes critical during pandemics. Organizations like the World Health Organization (WHO) play a central role in coordinating the global response, providing guidance, and facilitating the sharing of information. However, these organizations can also become points of contention. For example, during the COVID-19 pandemic, the WHO faced criticism from various countries regarding its handling of the outbreak and its relationship with China. Such criticisms can undermine the credibility of international organizations, making it more difficult to coordinate a global response.

Pandemics also highlight the disparities between nations, particularly in terms of healthcare infrastructure and access to resources. Low- and middle-income countries often suffer disproportionately during pandemics due to weaker health systems and limited access to vaccines and treatments. This disparity can exacerbate global inequalities and lead to long-term impacts on development and stability. The international community's response to these disparities, through mechanisms like the COVAX initiative, aimed at equitable vaccine distribution, is crucial in addressing these inequalities, but challenges remain in implementation and resource allocation.

In the longer term, pandemics can reshape global power dynamics. Countries that manage pandemics effectively can enhance their global standing, while those that struggle may see their influence wane. The response to pandemics can also lead to shifts in alliances, as countries seek to collaborate with others that share their interests in managing health crises. Additionally, pandemics can spur innovation and reform, leading to changes in how health systems are structured and how international cooperation is approached in future crises.

International Health Organizations (WHO, CDC)

International health organizations like the World Health Organization (WHO) and the Centers for Disease Control and Prevention (CDC) have important roles in managing global health issues. **These organizations are crucial in coordinating international efforts to combat diseases, respond to health emergencies, and promote public health on a global scale.**

The World Health Organization (WHO) is the leading international body responsible for global health. Founded in 1948 as a specialized agency of the United Nations, WHO's primary mission is to promote health, keep the world safe, and serve the vulnerable. The organization sets global health standards, provides guidance on public health issues, and coordinates international responses to health emergencies. For example, WHO was central in coordinating the global response to the Ebola outbreaks in West Africa and the Democratic Republic of Congo, helping to mobilize resources, provide technical expertise, and establish treatment protocols. WHO also has a key role in disease prevention through initiatives like vaccination campaigns and the promotion of healthy lifestyles.

The Centers for Disease Control and Prevention (CDC), based in the United States, is another key player in global health. While primarily focused on protecting public health within the U.S., the CDC also has a significant international presence. The agency works with health ministries and international partners to strengthen health systems, prevent infectious diseases, and respond to health threats worldwide. The CDC's Global Health Protection initiative, for instance, aims to build the capacity of countries to detect and respond to health threats, with a particular focus on preventing the spread of infectious diseases. The CDC also provides critical data and research that inform global health strategies, contributing to the broader understanding of public health issues.

Collaboration between WHO and CDC is essential for effective global health governance. These organizations often work together to address health challenges that transcend national borders, such as pandemics, emerging infectious diseases, and chronic health conditions. **During the COVID-19 pandemic, both WHO and CDC played significant roles in guiding global public health responses.** WHO coordinated international efforts, provided guidelines, and facilitated vaccine distribution through the COVAX initiative. Meanwhile, the CDC contributed through research, public health messaging, and direct assistance to countries struggling to manage the outbreak.

However, these organizations also face challenges, particularly in terms of funding, political pressures, and the complexity of coordinating international responses. WHO, for example, relies on contributions from member states and other donors, which can influence its priorities and actions. Political tensions can also affect the functioning of these organizations, as seen during the COVID-19 pandemic, when WHO faced criticism and scrutiny over its handling of the crisis and its relationship with member states. Similarly, the CDC's global role can be influenced by U.S. domestic politics and foreign policy considerations.

Health Diplomacy and Global Cooperation

Health diplomacy has emerged as a critical component of international relations, reflecting the recognition that health issues are intrinsically linked to global security, economic stability, and social well-being. **Health diplomacy involves the negotiation and implementation of international agreements, policies, and initiatives aimed at improving global health outcomes and addressing cross-border health challenges.**

One of the key aspects of health diplomacy is the role it plays in fostering global cooperation. In an interconnected world, health issues such as pandemics, antimicrobial resistance, and non-communicable diseases cannot be effectively addressed by individual countries acting alone. International cooperation is essential to managing these challenges, and health diplomacy provides the framework for such cooperation. This includes negotiations within international organizations like the World Health Organization (WHO), where member states work together to set global health agendas, share resources, and coordinate responses to health emergencies.

The COVID-19 pandemic is a stark example of the importance of health diplomacy. As the virus spread globally, it became clear that no country could manage the crisis in isolation. International cooperation was essential for sharing information about the virus, coordinating travel restrictions, and ensuring the equitable distribution of vaccines. Initiatives like the COVAX facility, which aimed to provide fair access to COVID-19 vaccines worldwide, were products of health diplomacy. These efforts required intense diplomatic negotiations to secure funding, manage supply chains, and address the needs of low- and middle-income countries.

Health diplomacy also has a role in peacebuilding and conflict resolution. In regions affected by conflict, health initiatives can serve as neutral grounds for dialogue and cooperation between warring parties. For instance, during the Ebola outbreak in West Africa, health workers were able to negotiate temporary ceasefires to allow for vaccination campaigns and the delivery of medical supplies. These efforts not only addressed immediate health needs but also contributed to broader peacebuilding processes by fostering trust and cooperation.

Another important aspect of health diplomacy is its role in promoting global health equity. Through diplomatic channels, countries can advocate for policies and initiatives that ensure all populations have access to essential health services, regardless of their economic or geopolitical standing. This includes efforts to reduce the price of essential medicines, increase funding for health systems in low-income countries, and promote the transfer of health technologies to developing nations. Health diplomacy thus becomes a tool for addressing global health disparities and advancing the right to health for all.

However, health diplomacy is not without its challenges. The intersection of health with other areas of international relations, such as trade, security, and human rights, can complicate diplomatic efforts. For example, negotiations over intellectual property rights for medicines often pit public health concerns against commercial interests, making it difficult to reach agreements that satisfy all parties. Additionally, political tensions between countries can spill over into health diplomacy, affecting cooperation on critical issues like pandemic preparedness and response.

Access to Medicines and Global Health Inequities

Access to medicines is a fundamental aspect of global health, yet significant inequities exist in the availability, affordability, and distribution of essential drugs across different regions of the world. **These disparities are a major concern in international relations, as they highlight the broader issue of global health inequities and the challenges of ensuring that all populations have access to the medical treatments they need.**

One of the primary factors contributing to global health inequities is the high cost of medicines, particularly in low- and middle-income countries. Many life-saving drugs, including treatments for HIV/AIDS, tuberculosis, and cancer, are priced beyond the reach of the world's poorest populations. The pricing of these medicines is often influenced by intellectual property rights, which grant pharmaceutical companies exclusive rights to produce and sell new drugs for a period of time. While these rights are intended to incentivize innovation, they can also limit access to affordable generics, particularly in developing countries.

The issue of access to medicines is further complicated by the global distribution of pharmaceutical production and supply chains. Many essential medicines are produced in a small number of countries, leading to vulnerabilities in the global supply chain. Disruptions in production, whether due to political instability, natural disasters, or pandemics, can lead to shortages and price increases, disproportionately affecting low-income countries. Additionally, the concentration of pharmaceutical production in certain regions can create dependencies, where countries without domestic production capabilities are reliant on imports, often at higher costs.

International efforts to address these inequities have included initiatives like the World Health Organization's (WHO) Essential Medicines List, which identifies the most important medications needed for a basic health care system. This list serves as a guideline for countries to prioritize their health spending and improve access to essential drugs. However, translating this list into actual access requires significant resources and political will, which can be lacking in many low-income countries. Furthermore, the challenge of ensuring that medicines are not only available but also affordable and of high quality remains a significant hurdle.

The issue of access to medicines has also been a focal point of global health diplomacy. Countries and international organizations have negotiated agreements aimed at improving access to affordable medicines, particularly in the context of global health crises. The 2001 Doha Declaration on the TRIPS Agreement and Public Health, for instance, affirmed the rights of countries to bypass patent protections in order to address public health emergencies, allowing for the production or importation of generic medicines. While this was a significant step towards improving access, the implementation of such provisions has been uneven, and the broader challenges of intellectual property rights in relation to public health continue to be debated.

The COVID-19 pandemic further highlighted the disparities in access to medicines and vaccines. High-income countries secured the majority of early vaccine supplies, leaving many low- and middle-income countries struggling to obtain doses. The COVAX initiative, led by WHO and other organizations, was designed to address this imbalance by providing vaccines to the most vulnerable populations globally. However, the challenges of funding, distribution, and political cooperation have limited the effectiveness of such efforts, illustrating the ongoing difficulties in achieving equitable access to medicines on a global scale.

CHAPTER 15: ETHICS AND MORALITY IN INTERNATIONAL RELATIONS

Moral Dilemmas in Global Politics

Moral dilemmas in global politics arise when decisions must be made that involve conflicting ethical principles, often with no clear right or wrong answer. **These dilemmas challenge policymakers to balance national interests with global responsibilities, human rights with security, and short-term gains with long-term consequences.** Each decision carries profound implications, not only for the countries directly involved but also for the broader international community.

One of the most prominent moral dilemmas in global politics is the question of humanitarian intervention. When a state engages in gross human rights violations, such as genocide or ethnic cleansing, the international community faces a difficult choice: Should they intervene militarily to stop the atrocities, even if it means violating the sovereignty of the offending state? The principle of state sovereignty is a cornerstone of international law, but so is the protection of human rights. This dilemma was starkly illustrated during the Rwandan genocide in 1994, where the international community's failure to intervene led to the deaths of hundreds of thousands of people. Conversely, the NATO intervention in Kosovo in 1999, aimed at preventing ethnic cleansing, was controversial because it bypassed the United Nations Security Council, raising questions about the legitimacy of such actions.

Another moral dilemma involves the use of drones in counterterrorism operations. Drones offer the ability to target terrorists with precision, minimizing the risk to military personnel and potentially reducing civilian casualties compared to traditional military operations. However, the use of drones raises serious ethical concerns, particularly regarding the legality of targeted killings, the potential for civilian casualties, and the psychological impact on communities living under constant drone surveillance. The secrecy surrounding drone operations, particularly in regions like the Middle East and South Asia, further complicates the issue, as it can lead to a lack of accountability and transparency.

Climate change presents another significant moral dilemma in global politics. The effects of climate change are felt worldwide, but the countries most responsible for greenhouse gas emissions are often not the ones that suffer the most from its impacts. This creates a moral obligation for wealthy, industrialized nations to lead efforts in reducing emissions and supporting vulnerable countries in adapting to climate change. However, these efforts can conflict with economic interests, such as the reliance on fossil fuels for energy and jobs, leading to difficult choices about balancing economic growth with environmental stewardship. The debates over climate change policies, both within countries and in international forums like the Paris Agreement, highlight the complexity of making ethical decisions that have global consequences.

The trade-offs between national security and individual freedoms also represent a moral dilemma in global politics. In the aftermath of terrorist attacks, governments often implement measures to enhance security, such as surveillance programs, travel bans, or detention of suspects without trial. While these actions can be justified as necessary for protecting citizens, they can also infringe on civil liberties and human rights. The balance between ensuring security and preserving individual freedoms is a contentious issue, as seen in the debates over the U.S. Patriot Act after the September 11 attacks or the use of mass surveillance by intelligence agencies around the world.

Global pandemics, such as COVID-19, further illustrate moral dilemmas in global politics, particularly concerning vaccine distribution. The question of who should get access to limited vaccine supplies raises ethical issues about equity and fairness. Should vaccines be distributed based on who can pay the most, or should they be allocated to those most in need, regardless of their country's wealth? The tension between nationalism and global solidarity in vaccine distribution reflects broader challenges in ensuring that global public goods are shared equitably.

These moral dilemmas highlight the complexity of decision-making in global politics, where ethical considerations must be weighed against practical realities. Policymakers are often forced to make difficult choices that have far-reaching consequences, navigating the delicate balance between competing moral imperatives.

Ethical Theories in IR

Ethical theories in international relations (IR) provide frameworks for understanding and evaluating the moral dimensions of global politics. **These theories help policymakers, scholars, and practitioners navigate complex issues, from war and peace to human rights and global justice.** The major ethical theories in IR include realism, liberalism, cosmopolitanism, and constructivism, each offering distinct perspectives on how ethics should influence international conduct.

Realism is one of the most influential theories in IR, often characterized by its pragmatic approach to ethics. Realists argue that the primary responsibility of states is to ensure their survival in an anarchic international system, where no central authority exists to enforce rules or norms. **In this view, ethical considerations are secondary to the pursuit of national interest and power.** Realists like Hans Morgenthau contend that moral principles cannot be applied universally in international politics because the nature of international relations is fundamentally different from domestic politics. **For realists, actions that might be considered unethical in a domestic context, such as deceit or coercion, may be justified if they serve the national interest or enhance state security.** This perspective often leads to the conclusion that international politics is governed by a different set of moral standards, where power and security are paramount.

Liberalism, in contrast, emphasizes the importance of ethical principles in guiding international relations. Liberals believe that international politics should be governed by the same moral principles that apply within states, such as justice, human rights, and the rule of law. Liberalism advocates for the creation of international institutions and norms that promote cooperation, peace, and the protection of human rights. The theory suggests that ethical considerations, such as the protection of individual freedoms and the promotion of democracy, should guide state behavior and international policymaking. Liberal thinkers like Immanuel Kant argued for the establishment of a federation of free states that would cooperate based on shared moral principles, reducing the likelihood of conflict and fostering global peace.

Cosmopolitanism extends the ethical concerns of liberalism beyond the state to the global level, advocating for a moral obligation to all humanity, regardless of national borders. Cosmopolitans argue that individuals, rather than states, are the primary subjects of moral concern, and that the international community has a duty to protect and promote the rights and welfare of all people. This perspective often leads to support for global governance structures and policies that prioritize global justice and the alleviation of poverty, inequality, and human suffering. Cosmopolitan thinkers like Martha Nussbaum and Thomas Pogge emphasize the importance of global solidarity and the need to address global injustices that transcend national boundaries. In practice, cosmopolitanism can lead to support for humanitarian interventions, global health initiatives, and efforts to combat climate change, all viewed as moral imperatives that demand collective action.

Constructivism, while not an ethical theory in the traditional sense, offers a unique perspective on the role of ethics in international relations. Constructivists argue that the international system is socially constructed, meaning that the norms, values, and identities that shape state behavior are created through social interactions and shared understandings. From this perspective, ethical norms are not fixed or universal but are shaped by historical, cultural, and social contexts. Constructivists like Alexander Wendt suggest that states' interests and identities are influenced by ethical norms, which evolve over time through interaction and discourse. This means that ethical considerations can change as states engage with one another, and that the international system is capable of moral progress as new norms, such as human rights, gain acceptance.

Each of these ethical theories offers valuable insights into the complexities of international relations. Realism provides a cautionary perspective on the limits of ethical action in a competitive world, while liberalism and cosmopolitanism emphasize the importance of ethical principles in guiding international conduct. Constructivism, meanwhile, highlights the dynamic nature of ethical norms and their influence on state behavior. Together, these theories provide a comprehensive framework for understanding how ethics intersect with power, interests, and global politics.

The Ethics of War and Peace

The ethics of war and peace is a central concern in international relations, involving deep questions about when, if ever, it is morally justifiable to go to war and how wars should be conducted. **Just war theory is the dominant framework used to evaluate the morality of war, providing criteria for determining whether the use of force is ethically permissible and guiding the conduct of military operations.**

Just war theory is divided into two main parts: jus ad bellum, which concerns the justification for going to war, and jus in bello, which deals with the ethical conduct of war. Jus ad bellum establishes criteria that must be met before a state can justifiably resort to war. These criteria include just cause, legitimate authority, right intention, probability of success, last resort, and proportionality. Just cause typically refers to self-defense or the protection of others from aggression. Legitimate authority means that only duly constituted authorities can declare war, while right intention requires that the aim of the war must be to achieve a just outcome rather than for reasons of self-interest or revenge. Probability of success ensures that the war has a reasonable chance of achieving its goals, and last resort dictates that all peaceful alternatives must have been exhausted before resorting to force. Proportionality demands that the anticipated benefits of the war must be proportionate to the expected harm.

Jus in bello, on the other hand, focuses on how war is conducted once it has begun. It includes principles like discrimination, which requires combatants to distinguish between military targets and civilians, and proportionality, which demands that the use of force in warfare must be proportionate to the military advantage gained. The principle of discrimination is critical in protecting non-combatants from the horrors of war, emphasizing that civilians should never be deliberately targeted. The proportionality principle in jus in bello also guards against excessive use of force that would cause unnecessary suffering.

However, the ethics of war and peace extend beyond just war theory to include considerations of pacifism and the moral implications of non-violence. Pacifism rejects war and violence entirely, arguing that ethical conflicts should be resolved through peaceful means, even in the face of aggression.

Pacifists argue that war inevitably leads to suffering and that it is morally wrong to take human life, regardless of the circumstances. While pacifism is often seen as an idealistic position, it raises important ethical questions about the human cost of war and the potential for non-violent alternatives to conflict resolution.

In recent years, the ethics of war and peace have also been challenged by new forms of warfare, such as drone strikes, cyber warfare, and the potential use of autonomous weapons. These developments raise complex ethical questions about the application of just war principles in modern conflicts. For example, drone warfare challenges the traditional understanding of discrimination and proportionality, as it often blurs the line between combatants and civilians and can result in unintended civilian casualties. Similarly, cyber warfare introduces new dilemmas about the proportionality of responses to digital attacks and the protection of civilian infrastructure.

The ethics of war and peace, therefore, require constant re-evaluation as the nature of conflict evolves. While just war theory provides a foundational framework for assessing the morality of war, ongoing developments in technology, warfare, and international relations demand that these ethical principles be continually reassessed to ensure they remain relevant and effective in promoting peace and justice.

Humanitarian Ethics and Global Intervention

Humanitarian ethics deals with the moral principles that guide actions aimed at alleviating human suffering, particularly in the context of global interventions. These interventions often occur in situations of armed conflict, natural disasters, or severe human rights violations, where the international community faces the challenge of deciding whether and how to intervene to protect vulnerable populations.

A key principle in humanitarian ethics is the concept of the "Responsibility to Protect" (R2P), which asserts that states have a duty to protect their populations from genocide, war crimes, ethnic cleansing, and crimes against humanity. When a state fails to do so, either through inability or unwillingness, the international community has a moral obligation to intervene, potentially including the use of military force. R2P represents a significant shift in the understanding of state sovereignty, placing the protection of human life above the traditional norm of non-interference in a state's internal affairs. This ethical framework has been invoked in various international crises, such as NATO's intervention in Libya in 2011, where the justification was to prevent imminent mass atrocities.

However, humanitarian interventions raise complex ethical dilemmas. One of the main concerns is the potential for such interventions to be used as a pretext for pursuing political or strategic interests rather than purely humanitarian goals. This can lead to questions about the legitimacy of the intervention and whether it truly serves the interests of the affected population. The intervention in Iraq in 2003, for example, was heavily criticized for being motivated by political considerations rather than humanitarian ones, despite the framing of the invasion as a means to liberate the Iraqi people from tyranny.

The principle of "do no harm" is also central to humanitarian ethics, emphasizing that interventions should not exacerbate the situation or cause additional suffering. This requires careful consideration of the potential consequences of an intervention, including the risk of escalating violence, destabilizing the region, or creating long-term dependency on foreign aid. For instance, the international intervention in Somalia in the early 1990s, initially aimed at addressing a humanitarian crisis, became entangled in the country's civil conflict, leading to significant casualties and a complex legacy of international involvement. This case underscores the importance of understanding the local context and ensuring that interventions are designed and implemented in a way that minimizes harm.

Humanitarian ethics also emphasizes the importance of impartiality, neutrality, and independence in delivering aid and conducting interventions. These principles are meant to ensure that humanitarian actions are guided solely by the needs of the affected population, without favoring any side in a conflict or being influenced by political agendas. **Maintaining these principles can be challenging in complex emergencies, where the lines between humanitarian and military objectives can become blurred.** For example, in Afghanistan, the integration of humanitarian aid into military strategies by some coalition forces led to criticism that aid was being used as a tool of war, potentially undermining the perceived neutrality of humanitarian organizations and putting aid workers at risk.

Humanitarian ethics, therefore, involves navigating a delicate balance between moral imperatives and the practical realities of intervention. While the intention to alleviate suffering and protect human rights is central to these efforts, the complexities of international politics, local dynamics, and the potential for unintended consequences require careful ethical deliberation. In the end, humanitarian interventions must be guided by a commitment to minimizing harm, respecting the dignity and rights of those affected, and ensuring that the actions taken truly serve the needs of the most vulnerable.

CHAPTER 16: FUTURE TRENDS IN INTERNATIONAL RELATIONS

The Impact of AI and Automation on Global Politics

The rise of artificial intelligence (AI) and automation is poised to reshape global politics in profound ways, influencing everything from military strategies to economic power dynamics. **AI's integration into various sectors of society has already begun to alter the balance of power, creating new opportunities and challenges for states as they navigate an increasingly digital world.**

One of the most significant impacts of AI on global politics is in the realm of military strategy and defense. AI technologies are being incorporated into weapons systems, surveillance, and cybersecurity, leading to the development of autonomous drones, advanced cyber warfare capabilities, and AI-driven decision-making tools. These advancements have the potential to change the nature of warfare, making conflicts faster and more precise, but also raising ethical and strategic concerns. For instance, the use of AI in autonomous weapons systems could lead to decisions being made without human oversight, increasing the risk of unintended escalation or errors in judgment.

AI is also reshaping intelligence and espionage. Machine learning algorithms can process vast amounts of data far more efficiently than humans, enabling states to analyze patterns, predict behaviors, and gain insights into the actions of other countries. This capability enhances the strategic advantage of states that can effectively deploy AI in their intelligence operations, but it also heightens the arms race in digital espionage, as nations seek to outpace each other in the development of AI-driven intelligence tools.

The economic implications of AI and automation are equally transformative. Automation is expected to disrupt labor markets globally, with certain jobs becoming obsolete while new industries and opportunities emerge. Countries that lead in AI research and development are likely to gain significant economic advantages, as AI-driven innovation boosts productivity and creates new markets. This could lead to shifts in global economic power, with states that invest heavily in AI technology potentially outpacing those that do not. However, the rapid pace of automation also risks exacerbating economic inequalities both within and between countries, as some populations may struggle to adapt to the changes brought about by these technologies.

AI's impact on governance and political decision-making is another critical area of concern. Governments are increasingly using AI to enhance public services, streamline administrative processes, and improve decision-making through data-driven insights. However, the use of AI in governance raises questions about transparency, accountability, and the potential for algorithmic bias. If not carefully managed, AI could reinforce existing inequalities and biases in society, leading to policies that disproportionately harm marginalized communities. Moreover, the centralization of data and control in AI systems could lead to more authoritarian forms of governance, where surveillance and control are enhanced through technological means.

On the international stage, AI could influence diplomatic relations and the balance of power between states. As countries compete for technological supremacy, AI could become a tool of soft power, with leading AI nations setting global standards and norms. This competition could lead to new alliances and rivalries, as states seek to align themselves with technological leaders or challenge them. Additionally, AI-driven propaganda and information warfare are becoming more sophisticated, with the potential to influence public opinion and disrupt democratic processes in other countries. The use of AI in these areas raises ethical concerns about the manipulation of information and the erosion of trust in democratic institutions.

In summary, the impact of AI and automation on global politics is multifaceted and far-reaching. These technologies have the potential to revolutionize military strategies, reshape economic power dynamics, and influence governance and diplomacy. As AI continues to develop, it will be important for states to navigate these changes carefully, balancing the opportunities offered by AI with the need to address the ethical, social, and political challenges that arise.

The Future of Global Governance

The future of global governance is shaped by the increasing complexity and interconnectedness of global challenges, requiring more adaptive and inclusive approaches. Traditional institutions like the United Nations (UN), the World Bank, and the World Trade Organization (WTO) were designed for a different era, and today, they face significant pressure to reform in order to remain effective. These institutions must evolve to address issues like climate change, cybersecurity, and global health, which transcend national borders and require collective action.

One key trend in global governance is the shift towards more inclusive and multi-stakeholder approaches. Non-state actors, including non-governmental organizations (NGOs), multinational corporations, and civil society groups, are playing an increasingly important role in global decision-making. These actors bring diverse perspectives and expertise, helping to address gaps in traditional governance structures. For example, in climate change negotiations, the involvement of NGOs and the private sector has been crucial in pushing for more ambitious commitments and innovations in sustainability.

Another important development is the rise of regional organizations and alliances. As global governance becomes more complex, regions are taking on greater responsibility for managing issues that affect their specific areas. Organizations like the European Union (EU), the African Union (AU), and the Association of Southeast Asian Nations (ASEAN) are increasingly active in addressing regional security, economic integration, and development challenges. These regional bodies can complement global efforts by tailoring solutions to local contexts and facilitating cooperation among neighboring states.

Technology is also transforming global governance, both as a tool for enhancing transparency and efficiency, and as a challenge that requires new forms of regulation. Digital platforms can facilitate global cooperation by connecting stakeholders across borders and enabling real-time communication. However, issues like data privacy, cybersecurity, and the regulation of emerging technologies like artificial intelligence (AI) present new governance challenges that traditional institutions are only beginning to address.

Challenges to International Order

The international order faces numerous challenges that threaten its stability and effectiveness. **These challenges stem from a variety of sources, including shifts in global power dynamics, rising nationalism, and the emergence of new global threats.** As the international system becomes more multipolar, with the rise of new powers like China and India, the traditional balance of power is being disrupted, leading to tensions and uncertainty.

One of the most significant challenges to the international order is the rise of populism and nationalism in many countries. This trend has led to a retreat from multilateralism and a focus on national sovereignty, often at the expense of international cooperation. In the United States, the "America First" policy under the Trump administration exemplified this shift, with a withdrawal from international agreements and organizations, such as the Paris Climate Accord and the World Health Organization (WHO). This trend is not limited to the U.S.; in Europe, the Brexit referendum reflected similar sentiments, where national interests were prioritized over regional integration. The rise of nationalism has weakened the foundations of the international order, as countries become more inward-looking and less willing to engage in collective action on global issues.

Another major challenge is the erosion of international norms and the rule of law. The post-World War II international order was built on a set of norms and rules designed to maintain peace and stability, such as respect for state sovereignty, human rights, and the peaceful resolution of disputes. However, in recent years, these norms have been increasingly challenged. Russia's annexation of Crimea in 2014, for example, violated the principle of territorial integrity and undermined the rules-based international order. Similarly, China's actions in the South China Sea, where it has built artificial islands and asserted expansive territorial claims, have raised concerns about the erosion of international maritime law. These actions set dangerous precedents, weakening the authority of international institutions and encouraging other states to flout international norms.

The proliferation of new global threats, such as cyberattacks, terrorism, and climate change, also poses significant challenges to the international order. These issues are transnational in nature and cannot be addressed by individual states alone, requiring coordinated international responses. However, the current international system is often ill-equipped to deal with these complex and evolving threats. For instance, the international community has struggled to develop effective norms and agreements to govern cyberspace, leaving states vulnerable to cyberattacks from both state and non-state actors. Similarly, efforts to combat climate change have been hampered by a lack of consensus among major powers and the difficulty of enforcing global agreements. These challenges highlight the limitations of the current international order in addressing the pressing issues of the 21st century.

Economic inequality and the uneven distribution of the benefits of globalization further exacerbate tensions within the international order. Globalization has lifted millions out of poverty, but it has also created significant disparities between and within countries. **These disparities have fueled social unrest and contributed to the rise of populist movements that challenge the existing order.** The backlash against globalization has led to a resurgence of protectionism and trade wars, as seen in the U.S.-China trade conflict, which threatens the stability of the global economy and undermines the rules-based trading system.

Finally, the rise of authoritarianism in some countries poses a direct challenge to the liberal values that underpin the international order. Authoritarian regimes, such as those in Russia and China, often reject the democratic norms and human rights principles that are central to the current system. These regimes have sought to expand their influence on the global stage, often through the use of economic and military coercion, challenging the dominance of Western democracies and the liberal international order they have championed. The competition between authoritarian and democratic models of governance is a fundamental challenge to the future of the international order, as it raises questions about the universality of the values on which the system is based.

Prospects for Global Peace and Security

The prospects for global peace and security in the 21st century are shaped by a complex interplay of factors, including the evolution of international power dynamics, the emergence of new security threats, and the capacity of the international community to manage and resolve conflicts. **While the end of the**

Cold War brought a period of relative stability, the current global environment is characterized by a range of challenges that threaten to undermine peace and security.

One of the key factors influencing global peace and security is the shifting balance of power in the international system. The rise of new powers, particularly China and India, alongside the relative decline of Western dominance, has led to a more multipolar world. This shift has introduced new uncertainties, as traditional power structures are challenged and new alliances are formed. While a multipolar world could potentially lead to a more balanced and inclusive global order, it also carries the risk of increased competition and rivalry among major powers, which could escalate into conflict. The ongoing tensions in the South China Sea, where China's assertive territorial claims have brought it into conflict with its neighbors and the United States, are a prime example of how shifting power dynamics can threaten regional and global stability.

In addition to traditional state-based conflicts, the nature of global security threats is evolving, with non-state actors playing an increasingly prominent role. Terrorism, cyberattacks, and organized crime are transnational threats that do not respect national borders and require coordinated international responses. The rise of groups like ISIS and the increasing frequency of cyberattacks on critical infrastructure highlight the challenges posed by non-state actors. These threats are difficult to address through conventional military means, requiring a combination of intelligence, law enforcement, and international cooperation. The ability of the international community to effectively manage these threats will be a key determinant of future global peace and security.

Climate change is another critical factor that will shape the prospects for global peace and security. As the effects of climate change become more pronounced, the potential for conflict over scarce resources, such as water and arable land, is likely to increase. Climate-induced migration could also lead to tensions as populations move in search of more hospitable environments, potentially exacerbating existing conflicts or sparking new ones. The international community's ability to mitigate and adapt to the impacts of climate change will be crucial in preventing these scenarios from leading to widespread instability.

The role of international institutions in maintaining global peace and security remains essential, but these institutions face significant challenges. The United Nations (UN), particularly the Security Council, has been criticized for its inability to effectively address some of the most pressing conflicts of the past decade, such as the Syrian civil war and the crisis in Yemen. Reform of international institutions to make them more representative and responsive to the current global landscape is often discussed but remains a contentious issue. The effectiveness of these institutions in adapting to new realities will be crucial in determining whether they can continue to play a central role in maintaining global peace and security.

Arms control and non-proliferation efforts are also vital to global security, particularly in preventing the spread of nuclear, chemical, and biological weapons. The erosion of key arms control agreements, such as the Intermediate-Range Nuclear Forces (INF) Treaty, and the uncertainty surrounding the future of the Iran nuclear deal, raise concerns about the potential for a new arms race. The proliferation of advanced military technologies, including drones and autonomous weapons systems, further complicates the security landscape, as these technologies can lower the threshold for conflict and make warfare more unpredictable. Strengthening arms control regimes and preventing the spread of these technologies will be essential for maintaining global peace and security.

APPENDIX

Terms and Definitions

- **Sovereignty**: The authority of a state to govern itself without external interference.
- **Nation-State**: A political entity characterized by a defined territory, stable population, and government; the state derives its legitimacy from representing a nation.
- **Diplomacy**: The practice of managing international relations through dialogue, negotiation, and other non-violent means.
- **Anarchy**: In international relations, a system in which there is no overarching authority above states; often used to describe the global system.
- **Balance of Power**: A theory in international relations suggesting that national security is enhanced when military power is distributed so that no single nation dominates.
- **Hegemony**: Dominance of one state or group of states in the international system, often through a combination of economic, military, and cultural influence.
- **Realism**: A theory in international relations that emphasizes the competitive and conflictual side of international relations, focusing on power and national interest.
- **Liberalism**: A theory in international relations that emphasizes cooperation, rule of law, international institutions, and the promotion of democracy and human rights.
- **Constructivism**: A theory that posits international relations are socially constructed through ideas, identities, and norms, rather than just material factors.
- **Multilateralism**: A diplomatic approach in which multiple countries work together on a given issue, often through international institutions.
- **Bilateralism**: Relations or policies involving two states, typically through direct negotiations or agreements.
- **Soft Power**: The ability to influence others through cultural or ideological appeal, rather than through military or economic pressure.
- **Hard Power**: The use of military and economic means to influence the behavior or interests of other political bodies.
- **Non-State Actor**: An individual or organization that has significant political influence but is not allied to any particular country or state.
- **International Law**: A body of rules established by treaty or custom and recognized by nations as binding in their relations with one another.
- **Treaty**: A formal, legally binding agreement between two or more sovereign states.
- **International Organization**: An organization composed of sovereign states or other intergovernmental organizations that works on common interests (e.g., the United Nations).

- **United Nations (UN)**: An international organization founded in 1945 to promote peace, security, and cooperation among countries.
- **NATO (North Atlantic Treaty Organization)**: A military alliance established in 1949 between North America and European countries for mutual defense.
- **European Union (EU)**: A political and economic union of 27 European countries that are located primarily in Europe.
- **ASEAN (Association of Southeast Asian Nations)**: A regional intergovernmental organization comprising ten Southeast Asian countries, promoting intergovernmental cooperation and economic integration.
- **International Monetary Fund (IMF)**: An international organization that aims to promote global monetary cooperation, secure financial stability, facilitate international trade, and reduce poverty.
- **World Bank**: An international financial institution that provides loans and grants to the governments of poorer countries for the purpose of pursuing capital projects.
- **World Trade Organization (WTO)**: An international organization dealing with the global rules of trade between nations, ensuring that trade flows smoothly, predictably, and freely.
- **Sanctions**: Commercial and financial penalties or other measures imposed on a country to influence its behavior in response to political or military actions.
- **Embargo**: An official ban on trade or other commercial activity with a particular country.
- **Peacekeeping**: The deployment of international military and civilian personnel to help maintain peace and security in post-conflict areas.
- **Humanitarian Intervention**: The use of force by one or more countries to prevent or stop widespread and severe human rights violations in another country.
- **Genocide**: The deliberate and systematic destruction of an ethnic, racial, religious, or national group.
- **War Crime**: A serious violation of the laws and customs of war, which can include atrocities such as genocide, mistreatment of prisoners, and the targeting of civilians.
- **Refugee**: A person who has been forced to leave their country in order to escape war, persecution, or natural disaster.
- **Asylum**: Protection granted by a state to a foreign citizen who has fled their own country due to fear of persecution.
- **Globalization**: The process by which businesses, cultures, and governments become interdependent on a global scale, driven by trade, communication, and technology.
- **Terrorism**: The use of violence and threats to intimidate or coerce, especially for political purposes.
- **Cybersecurity**: The practice of protecting systems, networks, and programs from digital attacks, which is becoming a major focus in international relations.
- **Nuclear Proliferation**: The spread of nuclear weapons and related technology to nations not recognized as Nuclear Weapon States by the Treaty on the Non-Proliferation of Nuclear Weapons (NPT).
- **Arms Control**: International agreements to manage or restrict the development, stockpiling, proliferation, and deployment of weapons.

- **Deterrence**: The strategy of preventing hostile actions by threatening significant retaliation, especially in the context of nuclear weapons.
- **Mutually Assured Destruction (MAD)**: A doctrine of military strategy in which the use of nuclear weapons by two or more opposing sides would cause the complete annihilation of both the attacker and the defender.
- **Non-Aligned Movement (NAM)**: An international organization of states considering themselves not formally aligned with or against any major power bloc.
- **Global South**: A term used to describe developing countries, particularly those in Africa, Latin America, and Asia.
- **Global North**: A term used to describe developed countries, particularly those in North America, Europe, and East Asia.
- **Sustainable Development**: Development that meets the needs of the present without compromising the ability of future generations to meet their own needs.
- **Human Rights**: Fundamental rights and freedoms that every person is entitled to, such as the right to life, liberty, and security.
- **Rogue State**: A state that is considered to be breaking international law and posing a threat to the security of other nations.
- **Proxy War**: A conflict where two opposing countries or parties support combatants that serve their interests instead of waging war directly.
- **Hybrid Warfare**: A strategy that blends conventional warfare, irregular warfare, and cyber warfare to achieve political objectives without triggering a full-scale war.
- **Soft Law**: Non-binding agreements, declarations, or standards that influence state behavior and international relations, without the legal force of treaties.
- **International Regime**: A set of implicit or explicit principles, norms, rules, and decision-making procedures around which actor expectations converge in a given area of international relations.
- **Collective Security**: The cooperation of several countries in an alliance to strengthen the security of each.
- **Civil Society**: The aggregate of non-governmental organizations and institutions that manifest interests and will of citizens, playing a role in global governance.
- **Humanitarian Aid**: Material or logistical assistance provided for humanitarian purposes, typically in response to crises including natural disasters and armed conflicts.
- **Trade War**: A situation in which countries try to damage each other's trade, typically by the imposition of tariffs or other trade barriers.
- **Diplomatic Immunity**: The privilege granted to diplomats that exempts them from the laws of the host country.
- **Extraterritoriality**: The state of being exempt from the jurisdiction of local law, usually as the result of diplomatic negotiations.
- **Geopolitics**: The study of the effects of geography (human and physical) on international politics and relations.
- **Sanctuary City**: A city that limits its cooperation with the national government effort to enforce immigration law.
- **Peacebuilding**: Efforts to establish lasting peace in post-conflict situations by addressing root causes of conflict and rebuilding institutions.

AFTERWORD

Congratulations! You've made it to the end of "International Relations in a Flash." We hope this journey through the field of global politics has been as enlightening for you as it was for us to create.

As you close this book, take a moment to reflect on how far you've come. From the basics of what international relations is all about, to the intricate theories that shape our understanding of global dynamics, you've covered a lot of ground. You've explored the balance of diplomacy, the high-stakes nature of international security, and the evolving global economy. You've grappled with weighty issues like human rights, environmental challenges, and the ethical dilemmas that world leaders face every day.

But here's the thing about international relations – it's not just about memorizing facts or understanding theories. It's about developing a way of thinking, a lens through which to view the world. The skills you've gained – critical thinking, analysis, and the ability to see issues from multiple perspectives – these are tools that will serve you well in many aspects of life, not just in understanding global affairs.

The world of international relations is constantly changing. The book you've just read captures a snapshot of our current understanding, but new events and developments are always reshaping the global landscape. Stay curious, keep asking questions, and don't be afraid to challenge existing ideas.

Whether you're a student looking to build a foundation for further studies, a professional seeking to better understand the global context of your work, or simply a curious mind eager to make sense of the world around you, we hope this book has given you insights and sparked your interest to learn more.

As you move forward, we encourage you to stay engaged with international affairs. Read the news with a critical eye, seek out diverse perspectives, and don't shy away from complex global issues. Your understanding and engagement matter – after all, in our interconnected world, we're all participants in international relations, whether we realize it or not.

Thank you for joining us on this journey through the essentials of international relations. We hope this book serves as a stepping stone for your continued exploration of our fascinating, complex, and changing world.

Made in the USA
Las Vegas, NV
15 December 2024

14337851R00081